ESSAYS
IN SOCIAL VALUES

BY

CLARENCE MARSH CASE

Essay Index Reprint Series

BOOKS FOR LIBRARIES PRESS, INC.
FREEPORT, NEW YORK

LIBRARY OF CONGRESS CATALOG NUMBER:
67-30201

Social Science Series Number Twenty-five

ESSAYS IN SOCIAL VALUES

A Volume in Appreciation
of
CLARENCE MARSH CASE
as
Teacher, Colleague, Friend

Sponsored by the Ph.D.'s in Sociology,
Other Graduate Students, and the
Faculty of the Department of Sociology,
The University of Southern California,
and by Other Friends of Dr. Case

Edited by Emory S. Bogardus

ESSAYS IN SOCIAL VALUES

PREFACE

This volume originated in a unanimous action taken at a joint meeting in July, 1944, of the Sociology Ph.D.'s and Faculty of the Department of Sociology of The University of Southern California. It represents a spontaneous expression of Dr. Case's graduate students and his colleagues in an effort to show their deep appreciation of his stimulating influence in their lives and their affectionate regard for a loyal friend, a brilliant teacher, and a scholar of the first rank.

The papers in this small volume have been selected from the articles and other materials from the pen of Dr. Case, most of which have been written since his latest book appeared. It represents the fourth unit in what may be regarded as a tetralogy of books in sociology. With *Non-Violent Coercion*, published in 1923, *Outlines of Introductory Sociology*, 1924, *Social Process and Human Progress*, 1931, and *Essays in Social Values*, 1944, the student will have available in handy form Dr. Case's major contributions to sociological thought. The bibliography of Dr. Case's writings, which appears at the close of the essays, will prove of special value.

The first essay presents Dr. Case's Social Age Trend Chart and is the only one of the group of essays that has not been published in periodical form. The chart at the conclusion of this essay is virtually a classification of values. It contains a classified exhibit of social values. A concrete exposition of the social age concept is found in the essay which follows on "The Social Infant on the Road." From a sociological viewpoint, the third essay, on the value concept, is perhaps the most important of the entire collection. The paper on "Conflict and Cooperation" brings out the social relationship between two great, underlying social processes. Then comes Dr. Case's exposition of his well-known conjuncture theory of leadership. Four essays follow on the subject of the machine and its effects on culture. The concluding three essays relate to the future of sociology, to the future of civilization, and to the future of peacemaking.

The papers as published in this volume were selected after consultation with Dr. Case. In order to conserve space in keeping with wartime restrictions, a few paragraphs from some of the essays have been omitted, with dots inserted to indicate the omissions.

The title *Essays in Social Values* is appropriate because most of Dr. Case's intellectual product easily falls under that heading. He has given special attention to the subject of social value in some of its pertinent aspects rather than to an analysis of what might be considered one specific social value after another. His writings have contributed to an important undertaking, namely, the elucidation of what is in reality of social value to mankind.

In dedicating this volume to our co-laborer, Dr. Case, the sponsors also wish to include Catharine Moore Case, for Mrs. Case continually played an integral and vital role in Dr. Case's lifework.

EMORY S. BOGARDUS
(For the Sponsors)

A TENTATIVE SOCIAL AGE TREND CHART*

SOMEWHAT MORE than a decade ago the present writer began to suspect that an uncharted factor in social behavior was working to upset sociological calculations. It seemed that the social behavior of many persons is not fully accounted for by chronological age, mental age, emotional age, or any other specific "age," or even the sum of these taken together. The social orbits of such persons do not run true to social form, but undergo perturbations in their courses not accounted for by age in years, physiological development, endocrine balance, mental performance, or that ratio between chronological age and mental age known as the "intelligence quotient." For example, men and women of mature years, robust physique, good emotional balance, and even superior intelligence quotient are found playing a glaringly childish part in the social situations of daily life. They are mature in terms of chronological, anatomical, physiological, and mental age, but have remained undeveloped and infantile in the field of overt social relations.

Definition of terms. In an article published in 1928, by the writer, the rather vague conception outlined above was called "social age," and under that name was more closely defined and somewhat fully illustrated.[1] The concept of social immaturity was therein also differentiated into two aspects, for which the terms "social infantility" and "social imbecility" were proposed. The writer further ventured at that time to affirm that social infantility is the disturbing factor, hitherto uncharted, in the social orbits of many who upset the orderly routine of community life with their unsocialized behavior.

Three years later (1931) the writer further defined and illustrated the concept in three chapters,[2] distinguishing social infantility from the term "social infantilism," which had

---

*In collaboration with Catharine Moore Case, and with the help of a score or two of graduate students at Stanford University, summer session, 1930, and in succeeding seminars at The University of Southern California.

[1]*Cf.* Clarence Marsh Case, "Social Imbecility and Social Age," *Sociology and Social Research*, 12:218-42, January-February, 1928.

[2]*Cf.* Case, *Social Process and Human Progress* (New York, 1931), chaps. VII-IX.

already been used by certain psychiatrists to indicate emotional undevelopment and immaturity, and also from such then current concepts as "social feebleness," and "social inadequacy." In the same chapters "social age" was distinguished from "developmental age" (a physiological factor) and, while not formally defined, was characterized as a form of social immaturity resting less upon physiological maturity or intelligence than upon disposition and habit, and as essentially a matter of socialized personality.[3] It was further pointed out in the book cited that the difference, not sufficiently made clear in the earlier article, between social infantility and social imbecility is that the socially immature and self-defeating behavior of socially infantile persons produces in the end the social imbecility of blundering, self-defeating groups. As now appears, it might make this distinction sharper if we were to speak of *social* infantility and *societal* imbecility. For example, the "grabbing" attitude so characteristic of both the chronological and the social infant, when generalized into group practice or policy, produces such societal imbecilities as aggressive international warfare, or the socially senseless growth of vastly swollen fortunes in the national life.

The logic of the above-reviewed groping exploration into this new subject had apparently thus netted, by the time indicated, the following results: (1) the notion of *social age* as a hitherto unrecognized factor in personal behavior in social situations; (2) the notion that social growth in this sense is a process of social-cultural conditioning; (3) the definition of "social infantility" as the status of those who have not matured in the social sense; (4) the definition of "societal imbecility" as the collective behavior of social infants and of those more socially mature persons who are compelled to pitch social policy on the infantile level of those social infants with whom they have to play the social game, if it is played at all in any democratic sense.

Objectifying the concepts. During the intervening years since the terms were thus defined, upon the basis of casual experience and sociological reflection, there has been a persistent effort on the part of the writer to test and amplify them by more systematic reference to objective facts. First of all

---

[3]*Ibid.*, pp. 137, 140.

arose the challenge of one's own mind: Are these really valid concepts, derived inductively from experience in the world of social fact, or simply convenient epithets for a criticism of social behavior from the viewpoint of personal preference and purely subjective evaluation? To this the answer seemed to be that, while primarily deductive and personally evaluative, the newly devised terminology actually rested on a basis of objective evidence in the social life going on around one. This factual basis seemed genuine, although insufficient; so that the logical situation seemed to call for a more sustained and critical effort to gather additional facts for and against the hypothesis. The line of procedure for such an attempt presented itself in the following form: If there really is such a thing as growth from a state or stage of social infancy to one of social adulthood, it would seem feasible to make a beginning by noting the social traits or attitudes of the chronological infant and contrasting them with those of the chronological adult. The task then became that of finding those traits which mark the behavior of chronological children, and which they tend to leave behind as they grow in years. Next, one would have to supplement this with a list of those traits or attitudes which mark the behavior of chronological adults of recognized social facility and acceptability — attitudes which they take on as they grow in years and social experience. Then one might arrange these traits or attitudes (whichever they are) in a continuous scale or array, beginning with the most clearly infantile and ending with those of the most grown-up quality. By so doing it might be possible to see whether the Apostle Paul's classic statement of spiritual growth applies also to growth in the social sense: "When I was a child, I spake as a child, I felt as a child, I thought as a child: now that I am become a man I have put away childish things."

The writer had already, in one of the chapters mentioned, singled out *mess-making*, *grabbing*, *squalling*, and *racketing* as distinctly infantile attitudes evident to anyone who has observed the behavior of young children. So there appeared as one task the extension of the list by observation and reflection, in person and through the work of others who had already published studies or who made them as advanced students cooperating in the present investigation. The list shown on the accompanying chart, along with this whole presentation itself, is highly tentative, and is published for illustrative purposes only. It uses the progressive form of the verb in every instance in order to provide uniform terminology and also to stress the fact that we are dealing here with general "tendencies to *act*" in the persons who may be referred to the chart for inventory.

This list of twenty-five attitudes was selected from a longer one, and was arranged in accordance with the writer's judgment concerning the relative degree of infantile or adult propensity for each of the behavior tendencies named on the scale. This personal judgment was checked against the judgment of others to the number of several hundred. These persons were asked to rank a jumbled list of the so-called traits with respect to their infantile, juvenile, or adult character. In so doing the traits were briefly defined as shown on the following ranking sheet, which (in jumbled form) was used with high school students, college students, and various adult groups.

A PRELIMINARY LIST OF BEHAVIOR TRAITS AND ATTITUDES SHOWING SOCIAL INFANTILITY AND SOCIAL MATURITY

(Numbers indicate a tentative ranking from the most infantile to the most mature)

1. Mess-making (failure to clean up after oneself)
2. Grabbing (seizing anything because one wants it right now and can get it)
3. Squalling (venting displeasure when grabbing is prevented)
4. Racketing (making needless noises for the fun of making them)
5. Smashing (wrecking things for fun or when angered)
6. Slapsticking (delight in seeing others tumble, sprawl, or meet other bodily mishap)
7. Monologuing (babbling to oneself)
8. Duologuing (babbling stimulated by the presence of others, but not addressed to them)
9. Dialoguing (talking to, and listening to, others)
10. Ordering (using language to affect the conduct of others)
11. Ego-Leading (leading others for the leader's own benefit)
12. Personal Criticizing (analyzing the conduct of others from one's own point of view)
13. Personal Opposing (blocking others for personal satisfaction)
14. Joining (the gang spirit, cliques, clubs, et cetera)
15. Social Conforming (behavior shaped by group pressure)
16. Honest Dealing (acting openly and dependably)
17. Truthtelling (speaking openly and dependably)

18. Fair Playing (seeking no advantage denied to opponents)
19. Peace Preserving (includes law observance, and more)
20. Altro-Leading (leading others for their benefit)
21. Social Opposing (pronouncing any act bad, not because the speaker dislikes it, but because it can be shown to be injurious to society)
22. Ethical Opposing (hostility toward principles rather than persons)
23. Nonconforming (refusing to yield to group dictation)
24. Conscientious Objecting (refusing, for conscience' sake, to obey the group will, but accepting punishment for so refusing without complaint)
25. Peacemaking (more creative than peace preserving; it fosters good will by doing justice)

Validity of the scale. It is not assumed here in the least that the scale has been validated by these rankings. Much less is it presented as quantitative in any statistical sense except in so far as it may represent a continuum in the looser sense of the term. It may be worth noting here that the rankings made by high school students agreed with that of the scale (which they had not seen) almost identically for the first half. Concerning the last twelve items there was much scattering. This fact the person giving this test in a high school very properly interpreted as reflecting the social inexperience and immaturity of students of that chronological age. They did not understand the definitions for the latter half, while they did understand the earlier half so well that the correspondence in our ratings was striking, as the collaborator[4] remarked.

It may not be amiss to point out a genuine progression or process of becoming as the scale runs from left to right. The first six items (Mess-making, Grabbing, Squalling, Racketing, Smashing, Slapsticking) indicate overt bodily behavior. Of these, the first three are especially characteristic of infants, while the last three are manifested as they grow stronger and more destructive. The entire six traits mark the stage of infancy and early childhood. The next seven (Monologuing, Dologuing, Dialoguing, Ordering, Ego-Leading, Personal Criticizing, Personal Opposing) deal largely with growth in the social uses of language. The remaining twelve (Joining, Social Conforming, Honest Dealing, Truthtelling, Fair Playing, Peace Preserving, Altro-Leading, Social Opposing, Ethical Opposing, Nonconforming, Conscientious Objecting,

---

[4]By W. G. Pierce as a teacher in Woodrow Wilson High School, Long Beach, California.

Peacemaking) involve the ethical aspects of the social life, in its wider humanitarian sense.

This is not, however, to say that the scale was arranged with any such progression in view. Far from that, the above-described grouping emerged logically from the nature of social life itself, and was recognized only after the attitudes were ranked in the order given on the chart, namely, that of their prevalence among children and adults, respectively.

The writer found some difficulty at the outset in determining whether these twenty-five characteristics should be called traits or attitudes; so both names were used in the title of the earlier list, a sample of which is reproduced herewith. Later it seemed best to follow the very clear distinction made by Professor Gordon W. Allport, who holds that *trait* is the more general of these two "indispensable concepts." While he recognizes that in some cases either term is correct, especially where *general* rather than specific attitudes are involved, he concludes: "The more generalized an attitude (the more difficult it is to specify its object or its polarity of affect), the more does it resemble a trait."[5]

In the tentative list as presented with this report it would seem that those items nearer the bottom of the list express more of that "chronic and temperamental" aspect of behavior which Allport would designate as a *trait*, or at least a highly generalized attitude. For instance, "social conforming" (No. 15) and "conscientious objecting" (No. 24) may be more specific, attitudinal aspects of the "ascendance-submission" directional scale which Gordon W. and Floyd H. Allport have used so ably in their studies of behavior in social conflict situations.[6]

Let it be further remarked that several of the terms in this list have been coined in the light of discussions and terms presented by various other writers. Thus the word *duologuing* is an adaptation of Piaget's "dual or collective monologue" in his admirable studies in Geneva, as reported by Thomas and Thomas in *The Child in America*.[7]

---

[5]*Cf.* Gordon W. Allport, *Personality: A Psychological Interpretation* (New York, 1937), p. 294.

[6]*Ibid.*, p. 298.

[7]William I. Thomas and Dorothy Swaine Thomas, *The Child in America: Behavior Problems and Programs* (New York, 1928), p. 535.

The terms *ego-leading* and *altro-leading* are the result of the present writer's attempt to reduce the quite similar concepts of Bogardus and Winkler-Hermaden to a common terminology uniform with that adopted in the attitude list herewith submitted. The practical equivalence of the "master" type of Winkler-Hermaden to the "autocratic" leader of Bogardus and of the former's "educator" with the latter's "democratic" leader was clearly stated by Paul Pigors in connection with a study made by him through the questionnaire method. By this means he drew out a set of responses from actual leaders which definitely sorted them into two types whose social maturity is expressed, in the conceptual framework of the present study, by our terms *ego-leading* and *altro-leading.*[8]

Social opposing is our term for that impersonal function of the good citizen, appraising acts in the name of the larger social welfare, so impressively explained by Professor Cooley.[9]

To Cooley we are indebted also for his discriminating chapter entitled "Hostility,"[10] from which is derived our term *ethical opposing.* Finally, our phrase *peacemaking* connotes a positive, constructive attitude not only immortalized in the New Testament beatitude, but recently analyzed by Professor David E. Henley in a sociohistorical study in which the term "creative peace-making" is given an extremely significant social role implying high social-ethical maturity.[11]

*The levels of social awareness.** Before the attitude list was completed the writer found himself speaking of *social*

---

[8]*Cf.* Paul Pigors, "Types of Leaders in Group Work," *Sociology and Social Research,* 21:3-17, September-October, 1936.

[9]*Cf.* Charles H. Cooley, *Social Organization* (New York, 1909), pp. 15 ff. and 201.

[10]Cooley, *Human Nature and the Social Order* (New York, 1902); entire chapter cited, especially pp. 271-76.

[11]*Cf.* David E. Henley, *The Society of Friends and Creative Peacemaking: A Study in Social Values* (doctoral dissertation, Department of Sociology, The University of Southern California, 1935).

*Being concerned with social awareness, this study differs somewhat from other studies in socialization, or sociation and social intelligence. *Cf.* W. A. Thomson, "Inventory for Measuring Socialization-Selfseeking, and Its Relationship to the Study of Value Tests," *Journal of Applied Psychology,* 25:202-12, April, 1941; L. D. Zeleny, "Measurement of Sociation, Social Status, and Adjustment," *American Sociological Review,* 6:173-88, April, 1941; F. S. Chapin, "Social Intelligence," *ibid.,* 7:214-28, April, 1942.—Editor's note.

awareness as the basic aspect of social growth. In like manner, this new concept soon divided itself into the three levels determined, respectively, by awareness of the *presence,* the *pleasure,* and the *welfare* of others.[12] These three levels would seem to call for some further explanation, especially since the writer regards them as the most significant aspect of the chart, a view which is shared by some of his colleagues and other associates. Continued reflection and considerable practice in the interpretation of social situations, particularly in a detailed and parallel study of the traffic problem, have made it plain that we have here one of the most useful keys to the explanation of human social behavior. Sociologically considered, the greatest moment in the experience of any individual is that one wherein he first becomes aware that there are *others,* that he is in a *social* world. One need not say that he comes on the instant to recognize it as of like kind with himself, since he may yet be unaware of himself as an individual. Apparently, he becomes conscious of himself as a *person* (as one aspect of a group) before he reaches consciousness of himself as a distinct unit defined over against the group (i.e., as an individual).[13]

In any case it is the high moment when his social life begins, a moment equaled in sociological significance only by that one in which he learns that his merely babbling vocal sounds can be used as means of communication with these newly found *others,* and also as an instrumentality for modifying their behavior.

The lowest section of the accompanying chart is called the level of "awareness of the presence of others." Its significance lies not only in the fact that it marks the beginning of social life with everybody, but in the further fact that with socially deficient persons it marks also the *end* of their progress in socialization. Probably only social idiots remain on that level for *all* social situations; for, inasmuch as dogs and

---

[12] In *Social Process and Human Progress,* p. 157. The writer has failed to notice these concepts in other writings, and either adopted them inadvertently from some forgotten source or originated them, without conscious intention in either case.

[13] J. Mark Baldwin's exposition of this dual process, *Mental Development in the Child and in the Race* (New York, 1915), was duplicated by Charles H. Cooley in various writings, and has since been corroborated by Read Bain, "The Self-and-Other Words of a Child," *American Journal of Sociology,* 41:767-75, May, 1936.

some other subhumans show awareness of the pleasure (and displeasure) of others, every normal human being may be expected to attain the lowest social level, which is marked only by awareness of the *presence* of others. Yet this holds true only in a general sense, for among human beings we find otherwise normal persons who display a glaring, even if not total, unawareness of the presence of others in various specific social situations. Familiar examples are those who absent-mindedly crowd other people off the sidewalk; or who plant themselves to hold lengthy conferences, during the pause between college classes, in the very doorways of buildings where hundreds of others are passing in and out with difficulty; or who park and unpark, drive and turn, in heavy traffic without regard or even awareness, in any social sense, that other drivers are on the road. Of course, in such cases there is not present a *total* unawareness of the *existence* of others, but merely a partial failure to be socially aware of their presence in particular fields and social situations. If one may borrow Sorokin's phrase just here, they do not perceive those others as in *social space*.

The second level, awareness of the *pleasure* of others, is the source and ground of companionableness, tact, and sociability. People with these traits have a superior degree of awareness with respect to the probable effect of their own words or actions on the feeling of others (tact), or a special fondness for being in the company of others (sociability), which means on the reverse side a more than average dislike of being alone.

The third level is awareness of the *welfare* of others. This is the stage of *socialization*, which means growth in capacity and willingness to take part in groups and to identify one's own welfare with the welfare of the group. As every student of elementary sociology knows, the merely sociable person may seek evil company for companionship's sake, or he may enjoy himself sociably at the expense of the larger social welfare. In a word, he may be sociable without being socialized, as Ross clearly showed in his *Social Control* as far back as 1901. The significance of this elemental sociological truth for the present discussion lies in the fact that the third great step in attaining social maturity consists precisely, as Ross pointed out, in passing on from companionableness to social responsibility in the larger sense; although it goes without saying that one never leaves the lower kind of social awareness behind when he goes on to a higher level. It is, of course, equally true that identification with a larger, wider group life may make it necessary for one to neglect participation, or even totally refuse it, in the activities of groups less inclusive in either their range of membership or their scale of values. For this reason diligence in "joining" groups can be no true measure or criterion of socialization, as has sometimes been assumed.

The groups. At the left of the chart appear eleven groups within whose progressively widening circle the drama of social growth goes on. These range from the family and play group to the nation and internation. These intersect each level of awareness, so that there is always visible a two-fold progression as the eye moves up the chart. This includes both an increasing sense of social awareness in the person himself and a more and more inclusive character in the groups which provide his stages of action. The names given these various groups are self-explanatory, with the possible exception of the "province," which word is used to indicate the divisions just below the nation itself, whether these be called provinces, or "states" as in this country.

The action patterns and their locations on the Social Age Trend Chart. As previously indicated, the action patterns are the overt behavior traits or attitudes of individuals under observation. Any form of conduct or reaction which exhibits a degree of social infantility or social maturity, and is recognizable as such, may be recorded on the chart.

The small rectangles into which the face of the chart is divided are used to mark the locations of specific acts or *"action* patterns" of a person to whose behavior the chart is applied. In such a test a useful procedure is first to record the various acts on a separate guide sheet, or use the reverse side of the chart itself, numbering them in the order of appearance to the observer, and placing the numbers in the appropriate squares, opposite the traits which most appropriately designate them and also opposite the appropriate **groups** indicated on the left of the chart, taking care that they are recorded on the proper levels of awareness. If the same type of behavior is observed at different times, this fact may be indicated on the work sheet and transferred to the chart when the analysis is completed. For instance, if item No. 1 is observed three times, that is, the behavior is repeated three times on successive occasions, this fact may be indicated by recording 1+3.

To illustrate the use of the chart, several forms of behavior may be given and recorded. Suppose a small child is observed to be a mess-maker at home. He is aware of the presence of others, but there is no indication that he is interested in the pleasure or welfare of others. The item is recorded, but since this is the first observation made, the figure 1 is placed in the lower left-hand corner, in the square under mess-making and opposite the "family" group. Later the child is observed grabbing a toy owned and held by a playmate, and in the end taking it away from the playmate and breaking it to pieces. Whereupon the playmate begins squalling. Two forms of behavior of the first child are observable — grabbing and smashing. Since these acts take place in a play group, the items (2 and 3) are recorded under "grabbing" and "smashing," respectively, and on the second line from the bottom opposite "play group." The squalling by the child whose toy was smashed may be recorded as the first observed mode of behavior of the second child, using a separate chart to record this behavior under "squalling" on line two from the bottom of the page.

Taking the case of a mature adult, as shown by his earnest concern about the outcome of the war and of the future peace, we can observe a different set of behavior traits. This person participates actively in a movement at great sacrifice to himself to bring about a just peace and to establish a new world order to guarantee lasting peace. In his behavior he shows a strong sense of social responsibility, not only to his country but to the world beyond the boundaries of his country. He is not standing idly by but acts in what he conceives to be the most effective way of getting results. This act, or series of acts, may be recorded in the upper right-hand corner under "peacemaking" and opposite "internation."

What the chart measures. The chart measures the more or less clearly observable forms of behavior that are subject to classification. However, sometimes it is not easily possible to indicate exactly on what level the behavior occurs. The behavior reaction to a social situation is so complex that only an approximate classification is possible. If there is too much uncertainty about the behavior, particularly in regard to the possible motive behind the act, the specific item cannot be recorded. But there are sufficient classifiable forms of behavior to get a fairly accurate profile of a person's behavior traits, provided the subject is observed over a long enough period.

Let it be repeated that the chart as it stands is not designed to measure exact items in a quantitative sense, but it is believed that we have here a sort of pictorial inventory of the trend of a person's behavioristic progression toward social maturity. This would be indicated by the position of the squares checked for his actions, as observed above. The ideal progression or profile is a diagonal line, or band, of action patterns running from lower left-hand corner to the upper right-hand corner. An infantile person, that is a chronological infant or a socially imbecile adult, would display action patterns limited to the three or six attitudes or traits at the left and on the lowest awareness level. On the other hand, a highly socialized person, chronologically either young or old, would score heavily in the upper squares. In other words, the social infant expresses the less mature attitudes, in the smaller, more intimate, groups, and upon the lowest level of social awareness, so that his action patterns are clustered in the lower left area of the chart. The social adult is not so closely limited, ranges more widely over the chart, but scores most heavily with the more mature attitudes, within the more inclusive groups, and upon the higher level, namely, that of awareness of the welfare of others. The scorings for these clusters in the upper right area of the chart do not mean that a person has abandoned the other levels of awareness; for a full-grown, mature adult may at times exhibit behavior which normally might be expected to appear during early childhood, and would be indicated on the left side of the chart, and possibly in the lowest level of awareness.

If desired, this chart can be used to study the development of a person over a period of years, especially by dating observations on the work sheet, and then using some device of indicating this on the chart.

While the chart thus far worked out is extremely crude and nonmathematical and nonquantitative, it seems to have a diagnostic, therapeutic value which has won for it the hearty approval of those who have applied it. Those who have applied the chart to themselves, or have cooperated with the observers of the subjects (the cooperators), have been able to observe their own progress in behavior. The observers have testified that they have noticed marked changes in the social behavior of the subjects under observation. Mutual scoring by members of the family may produce a by-product wholly outside the strictly analytic and objective observation of behavior. That there should be such a socially therapeutic property about this social diagram is not hard to explain.

SOCIAL AGE TREND CHART
by
CLARENCE MARSH CASE

Column headings (left to right):

MORE INFANTILE TRAITS: Mess-making, Grabbing, Squalling, Racketing, Smashing, Slapsticking, Monologuing, Duologuing, Dialoguing, Ordering, Ego-Leading, Personal Criticizing, Personal Opposing, Joining, Social Conforming, Honest Dealing, Truthtelling, Fair Playing, Peace Preserving, Altro-Leading

ADULT TRAITS: Social Opposing, Ethical Opposing, Nonconforming, Conscientious Objecting, Peacemaking

LEVEL III—Awareness of the Welfare of Others

	Internation	Nation	Province	Civic Community	Occupational Group	Casual Group	School	Church	Neighborhood	Play Group	Family

LEVEL II—Awareness of the Pleasures of Others

	Internation	Nation	Province	Civic Community	Occupational Group	Casual Group	School	Church	Neighborhood	Play Group	Family

LEVEL I—Awareness of the Presence of Others

	Internation	Nation	Province	Civic Community	Occupational Group	Casual Group	School	Church	Neighborhood	Play Group	Family

THE SOCIAL INFANT ON THE ROAD

IT IS NOT NECESSARY to spend many words painting the serious nature of the traffic problem. It is great and growing, as all who think are aware. It is also widely recognized that very little headway is being made to solve it, in spite of the earnest and able efforts of a great many people, official and unofficial.

Following Professor Charles A. Ellwood's lead, sociologists have often pointed out that there is at bottom only one single social problem, and that is the problem of *living together*. The traffic problem is, therefore, simply the problem of living together on the streets and highways. And let us say at the outset that millions of people are not fully fit to meet the requirements of that sort of living together. As Professor W. F. Ogburn has expressed it, we are merely cave men trying to live in the modern city. We are equipped with a brand of human nature that fails to measure up to the demands of the civilized situation, which is a very recent one as far as the experience of our race is concerned. In no sphere of human interest has our social immaturity shown itself more crudely than in its failure to socialize the machine economy in general. And within that technological situation itself, our crude, barbarian infantility shows itself most plainly in the vast swarms of social infants romping through our streets and along our highways with magnificent motor cars which their drivers are utterly unfitted to use in a truly social manner. Not that they are guilty of evil intent. They are merely bent on pleasing themselves, just like any other juvenile with his glittering Christmas toy. In the general scramble to grab the most for one's little self out of the machine economy in general, "we injure ourselves more with our elbows than we do with our fists," as Professor C. H. Cooley happily phrased it. Likewise, absorbed in our entrancing automobiles, we shove or catapult one another off the road, not from any desire to do so, but in the service of a childish mania for getting there first, or for getting nowhere in particular faster than anybody else.

When I say "we" in this connection, I do not mean that all are equally guilty. On the contrary, it became very clear at the outset of my own traffic studies, ten years ago, that most of the trouble on the road is caused by less than one tenth of the drivers. Many other students of the subject have arrived at the same conclusion. Of course, there is an element of guesswork in such reasoning because of the fact that statistics are insufficient, and in view of the fleet, and even flitting, nature of the specimens we have to observe whenever we try to investigate traffic behavior. In other words, we need life histories of dangerous or merely troublesome drivers. By this I mean we should have accurate records of their driving experiences and their own attitudes toward traffic laws and situations and toward themselves as drivers. The writer has made careful, first-hand observations of many thousands of situations, based on nearly a hundred and fifty thousand miles of touring in thirty-three states of this Union. Several scores of collaborators have conducted interviews or written accounts of motoring experiences, and placed them at our disposal. All this sociological evidence leads straight· to the conclusion that a large but undetermined number of drivers are unfit by reason of their personality traits to drive an automobile, and should not be allowed to do so.

At the same time, psychologists have approached the problem from their own point of view and method of study. This led them to single out the individual driver and take him into the laboratory, where they measured his sense reactions by means of elaborate machinery. They tested his vision for clearness, depth, and width of field, his sense of color, his quickness of movement or reaction time, his tendency to move about on the seat and to turn his head or to sit motionless. These and other traits they related to his accident rate, and attempted to draw certain conclusions as to his fitness to drive in traffic. Some of the most notable of these studies were made at Ohio State University and they have been of considerable value. Nevertheless, such researches are hampered by a fatal weakness, namely, that the experimental conditions set up in the psychological laboratory are not the same as those under which driving in traffic is actually carried on. For one thing, in the laboratory the individual being examined is required to keep his eyes on a dial attached to the instrument board close to him.

But in the real traffic situation of the street he has to watch large objects moving at a distance, and in several directions at the same time; and he certainly does not watch his instrument board if he knows anything about driving. These limitations of their method have been partially recognized by the psychologists themselves, apparently more clearly than many laymen who have pinned entirely too much faith in the value of such studies for a solution of this serious traffic problem. We are still faced, after all our measuring of the nervous systems of drivers, colored lights, and signboards, with the same old problem in ever-growing dimensions.

The sociologists from the start were aware of this weakness in the method of the psychologist, and for their own part attempted to make their studies in the actual stream of traffic which flows endlessly along our streets and highways. The social psychologists likewise betook themselves to the crossroads, where some very significant observations have been made, particularly by Professor Floyd H. Allport, with respect to behavior in the face of the signal bell on the part of drivers of different personality types. Yet all sociological researches are plagued by their own inherent weakness of method, just as were those of the laboratory psychologist. The weakness, however, points in opposite directions in the two cases. The psychologist in the laboratory makes very accurate measurements but does not succeed in measuring the actual behavior with which we are concerned. On the other hand, the sociologist out on the road is a participant observer in the actual driving situation, but for that very reason cannot follow up his human specimens and analyze them with sufficient accuracy. In a word, the two sciences together have succeeded only in studying the unreal situation very accurately, and the real situation quite inaccurately. Meanwhile the slaughter goes on, the perpetrators of that very large proportion of it which is not accidental in the true sense go undetected beforehand and usually unpunished in any effective way afterward. Such is the situation as we now face it after more than a third of a century of effort and exhortation.

The one thing that has been discovered by all observers is that a relatively few drivers are causing most of the mischief. At the same time, the most striking fact about the traffic

situation is the skill and consideration with which the millions
of cars one sees in a transcontinental tour are handled by the
vast majority. The small band of mischief-makers include,
aside from children, who should not be expected or allowed
to drive, those who are intoxicated with alcoholic beverages in
greater or lesser degree and the genuine Road-Mutt. Leaving the drunken driver aside for this occasion, let us notice the
last-named group. I have called them Road-Mutts because
they seem to fill on the road the same role carried by Mutt
in the well-known comic strip of the daily press. Mutt in the
cartoon is not the enemy of Jeff by any means, but he has a
way of imposing on his companion and occasionally shoving
him around, which suggests a crude and unsocialized personality. "We injure one another more with our elbows than
with our fists"; and Mutt, whether figuring in the comic strip
or the anything-but-comic traffic accident, is no exception to
the rule. The main trouble is that he is unfit to manage a
motor vehicle and should not be permitted to do so. Thinking
especially of these Mutts, it was said in opening that our
human nature is of a sort that does not fully meet the requirements of the modern civilized, technological world, particularly that situation created by our powerful and potentially
dangerous motor-driven vehicles. But this does not imply
that human nature is unchangeable. Nobody believes that
less than the sociologist. His studies of actual social life have
taught him that human behavior is largely the expression of
attitudes, or tendencies to act. These are themselves largely
the product of experience and training in such groups as the
family, play group, neighborhood, school, church, and civic
community. In them human nature is largely made, and in
and through their agency it can be remade. For this very
reason, namely, that they are not doomed by fate to remain
that way, we should now mightily resolve to weed the Road-
Mutts out of the motoring life of our cities and country highways. The delinquent driver of this type is deficient in his
attitudes, his disposition, his appreciation of the fact that
good and safe driving is a matter of being sufficiently aware
of the presence, the pleasure, and the welfare of others. He
does not recognize that every man is in a sense his brother's
keeper; that traffic behavior especially, if it is to become what
it should be, is a matter of mutual aid.

It will be recognized that all these are *social traits*. They grow out of the process of living together, and they alone make a better way of living together possible of attainment. Those who are not socialized in this sense are really not yet grown up, although they may be matured six-footers with bushy whiskers, or even silvery heads. Despite these and all other surface signs of full manhood, they are really *social infants*, as earlier defined by the present writer;[1] and driving in modern traffic is no fit task for infants, whether chronological or social. If we do not weed them out of our traffic, we shall demonstrate that there is a strain of social imbecility, if not infantility, in all of us, and consequently in the community itself. The question now is how to do it.

The psychological and sociological investigations mentioned above were made partly in the hope of devising some set of tests by which it would prove possible to examine applicants for the driver's license and prevent the unfit from being turned loose on the highway. But that has been rendered impracticable by our failure to perfect a sound set of tests, by the expense involved, and by the vast amount of time that would be required to administer it. . . . .

The present argument holds that average human nature has mental and social limitations which the enormous elaboration of swift machinery in general is placing under drafts that tax it beyond its ability to manage. Although human nature is very plastic, and perhaps even now changing before our eyes, that does not prevent a very serious lag for the time being. The common man, to say nothing of the children, has never wielded such powerful and dangerous playthings before; yet he persists in handling them after the patterns of the horse-and-buggy days, including the habit of driving each for himself, and without adequate awareness of others and of the supremely *social* nature of the act, which is really social in a way and degree never experienced before in the daily activities of ordinary life. The degree of self-control, self-subordination, and discipline required in driving correctly had been reserved hitherto for the conduct of armies and navies, lion hunting, arctic exploration, and other hazardous

---

[1]*Sociology and Social Research*, 12:218-42, January-February, 1928; also *Social Process and Human Progress* (New York, 1931), chaps. VII-IX.

enterprises involving either a great many people together or
a few in especially hazardous undertakings. The outcome of
all this wholesale turning loose of socially immature drivers
in modern traffic is that the vast majority of so-called "accidents" are not really accidents at all, but simply *consequences*.
An *accident* is any event that happens unexpectedly and which
is not taking place according to the usual course of things. A
consequence, on the contrary, is a natural and necessary result
which ensues from any set of causal conditions. Presumably
everything happens from some cause, regarded in the scientific sense, but in the popular and practical sense, as here
used, the distinction is valid. I suppose the distinguishing
criterion is that a consequence might be easily forecasted by
anyone with normal foresight, whereas a true accident cannot be foreseen, and hence may not be avoided. The application to traffic problems is that the vast majority, as already
remarked, of our mounting traffic disasters are not really accidents, but are consequences that could easily be forecasted
and avoided. In view of the combination of drivers with
unsocialized dispositions, aspiring to manage more and more
powerful cars, upon faster and faster roads, the present
appalling destruction of property, limb, and life is exactly
what should be expected. We need a new word for such
things, for they are not accidents, although "consequences"
may strike one as too academic.

The present motoring system turns loose upon the highways many a driver whose only salvation lies in the chance
that he may not run afoul of another of his own kind. Such
persons are *minus* or *delinquent* drivers, who constantly fall
short of the social requirements and come back from every
trip with a lot of unpaid social obligations. Over against
them stand the *plus* or *master* drivers, who do better than the
average and help rather than hinder those whom they meet
upon the road, whether other automobilists, pedestrians, or
officers of the law. They often return with a balance to their
credit, having done even more than the letter of the law requires. Between these two classes is the mass of average
drivers who play the game as required, but take no special
pride in meeting the higher social and ethical challenge of the
traffic situation. Such a sportsmanlike spirit can, however,
be aroused by safety campaigns and other educative efforts,

so that the two following avenues are open for improving the situation. One is to eliminate the delinquent drivers from the road, and the other is to convert drivers who merely drive as required by the routine into master drivers, animated with the ambition to do this difficult and dangerous thing of motoring with a really artistic finish.

If this seems fantastic and impossible, it is so merely because the mental and social level of drivers is low, and this low level, especially the social, may be merely the result of inadequate social control. In other words, there remain too many horse-and-buggy drivers behind automobile steering wheels. This applies more directly to older drivers, who are still under the habits of the preautomobile folkways. It applies to younger drivers only indirectly, since they never experienced the horse-driving complex, and share its folkways only by virtue of the fact that young drivers usually drive, with some startling variations, according to the patterns set by their elders. The same thing may be stated in terms of motoristways, by saying that these are now in process of formation. People have no sufficiently clear conception of the situation this swift machine has clapped down upon us, and no clear and definite picture of the kind of groupways required to meet it well. The net result is that many drivers, particularly the younger ones, possess no clear pattern, either as folkways or as motoristways, and that leaves too much opportunity for each to try being a law unto himself. This impulse is further aggravated in the case either of those who are too young in years to possess the necessary discretion or of those who, by defect of nature or training, lack the matured social disposition of cooperation and mutual aid, and consequently remain social infants, of low social age, regardless of their weight of years. . . . .

Just here, in the unsocialized driver old or young, lies the central difficulty of modern traffic, and toward this conviction there has been a steady convergence of all who have approached the problem from its various sides, which are many and important. But as it now stands in the light of the resulting consensus of opinion, it is a *social* problem, both in its essential nature and in the methods that must be applied for its solution. It is unnecessary to quote the numberless speakers and writers who have spotted the driver as the central and most stubborn root of the difficulty. The *vehicle* itself cannot, of course, resist when streamliners propose to convert it from the thing of beauty which it now is into something resembling a colossal football on wheels. The *highway* can utter no protest when it is engineered from a winding, contoured, common way, an integral, friendly part of the landscape—like Whitman's "long brown path before me leading wherever I choose"—into a wide, straight groove for madly rushing speedsters, detached, like this highway itself, from the roadside life and oblivious to its charms. But when it is proposed to change the *driver*, to socialize and regiment him in the ways that must be practiced, his intractableness under the pressure of social engineers is matched only by the docility of the other two factors in the hands of the mechanical and civil engineers.

At this very point, nevertheless, the problem comes to be more clearly defined, and that is a real gain. It reached that stage in this country when articles began to multiply in popular magazines under such titles as "Dangerous Fools," "The Killers—A Challenge to American Business," "Telling It to the Judge," "Tremendous Trifles," and "Worse Than War." This group of titles is a mere random sample indicative of a vast literature on this problem. Its sociological meaning is that a considerable number of competent observers have become aware of the essential nature of these evil conditions, and there is a growing consciousness of the necessity of seeking a remedy by collective action of some sort. In other words, traffic has reached that stage in the public, or social, mind which elevates it to the position of a real social problem. To become aware of it as socially bad is the first stage; to analyze it for its factors is the second; and the third is to find that solution, which, by virtue of the very fact that it is a *social* problem, cannot be found by individual action alone.[2] . . . .

We in these days are prone to think of the problem as one of motor vehicles exclusively, but it is much older and wider than that. An authority in traffic studies has remarked

---

[2] As defined by the present writer elsewhere, a social problem means any social situation which attracts the attention of a considerable number of competent observers within a society and appeals to them as calling for readjustment or remedy by social, i.e., collective, action of some kind or other.—*Outlines of Introductory Sociology* (New York, 1924), p. 627.

the fact that "ancient cities as well as modern suffered from
street congestion. Caesar found it necessary (in ancient
Rome) to issue an order prohibiting the passage of wagons
through the central district for 10 hours after sunrise."[3]
The same problem aroused William Phelps Eno in his pioneer studies of street congestion in New York City. That
was in 1899 before the automobile was a factor, Eno's original impetus having come from vexatious delays to carriages
at the breaking up of opera crowds in that city. So one
readily sees that here is a problem that springs up peren-
nially wherever great numbers of vehicles attempt to use
the same streets, and it is not tied up to any particular kind
of vehicle or type of street. In the opening sentences of his
classical work on *Social Control,* published nearly forty years
ago, Professor E. A. Ross used these significant words:

A condition of order at the junction of crowded city thoroughfares
implies primarily an absence of collisions between men or vehicles that
interfere one with another. Order cannot be said to prevail among
people going in the same direction at the same pace, because there is
no interference. It does not exist when persons are constantly colliding
one with another. But when all who meet or overtake one another in
crowded ways take the time and pains needed to avoid collision, the
throng is orderly. Now at the bottom of the notion of social order lies
the same idea.[4]

As the book quoted goes on to show in a masterly way,
the achievement of order, as defined, in the various fields
of associated activity, is the task of *social control,* and this
is made possible by the fact that "from the interactions of
individuals and generations there emerges a kind of collective mind evincing itself in living ideals, conventions,
dogmas, institutions, and religious sentiments which are
more or less happily adapted to the task of safeguarding
the collective welfare from the ravages of egoism."[5]

This states exactly the colossal task to which, under the
leadership of Herbert Hoover, the National Conference on
Street and Highway Safety set itself in 1924. The "ravages
of egoism" had piled up such a shocking toll of serious and
fatal accidents that something had to be done to protect the

---

[3]Miller McClintock, *Street Traffic Control* (New York, 1925), p. 2.
[4]Edward A. Ross, *Social Control: A Survey of the Foundations of
Order* (New York, 1901), p. 1.
[5]*Ibid.,* p. 293.

collective welfare along that line. Again, just as Ross phrased it some decades before, there was the interaction not only of individuals, but of generations, at work in the matter. This process had registered itself in the *folkways*, already quite familiar in all sociological discussion; and out of the interaction of living individuals with their contemporaries and with their forerunners must be evoked that new "sort of collective mind" which would be better prepared to deal with this new form of an old problem, created by the extraordinary spread of the automobile. During the years of its existence the National Conference has been striving in a systematic way to assist the public mind in forming the living ideals, conventions, and institutions demanded by the situation; and that is the process of creating *motoristways* which has been emphasized throughout the pages of this article.

All these efforts are expressions of numberless agencies and individuals that need not, and cannot, be named, but all are working at the one great task of creating the collective mind of the new motoristways, whose function is that of "safeguarding the collective welfare from the ravages of egoism" or, in our present terminology, from the dangerous antics of the social infant on the road.*

---

*Reprinted from *Sociology and Social Research*, 23:3-17, September-October, 1938.

THE VALUE CONCEPT IN SOCIOLOGY AND RELATED FIELDS*

ONE MIGHT BE justified in saying that the word "values" has been used with greater precision in economics than in other fields of social study. But it would have to be added that its very precision in that case reduced it to a relative poverty of connotation which limited its usefulness as a key to the interpretation of the larger social life. This deficiency was perceived by B. M. Anderson, and in his able pioneer work, *Social Values,* he went a long way toward overcoming it. But in so doing his rather large dependence on sociological ideas made it clear that a concept so basic for the explanation of all social life naturally falls to the task of sociology. . . . .

Professor C. H. Cooley's chapters on "Valuation" in his *Social Process* are the work of a mind well trained in economics and philosophy as well as in sociology. So we here accredit in part to economics those chapters, which are distinguished by their firm grasp of this value concept in both these social sciences and their interrelations.[1]

In economics, as also in philosophy and perhaps in music and graphic art, the idea of value has shown a tendency toward an exclusively positive connotation. In economic discussions it signifies something desirable, namely, a "utility," which in turn is a thing or a service "capable of satisfying human wants." A utility in the general sense is, as its name suggests, always useful and, therefore, desirable; which is to say that it is a *positive* value in the generic sense. Economic utilities, or goods, are both desirable and scarce, and it is this combination that makes men willing to give even distasteful effort for them. The economic good is thus defined as a positive value, or desirable object.

While the term "disutility" appears in economic literature, it has not filled a very important place and seems almost incidental. Alfred Marshall's *Principles of Eco-*

---

*Address delivered in part at the Tenth Annual Meeting of the Pacific Sociological Society, which met at the University of California, December 28-30, 1938.

[1]Charles H. Cooley, *Social Process* (New York, 1918), chaps. XXV-XXVIII.

nomics makes no use of it. Although his work was an advanced exposition of neoclassic economic theory, Richard T. Ely's very widely used *Outlines of Economics* likewise presents nothing on "disutility," while it seems to admit that economic values are all positive in the following passage: "Economic wants may be serious, frivolous, or even positively pernicious, but the objects of these wants all alike possess utility in the economic sense." Utility he has already, defined as "power to satisfy wants." As utilities they are all good, despite the fact that the wants which they satisfy may be even "pernicious" in some larger frame of social or moral reference. It appears that economic theory thus implicitly defines its values in positive terms only, and so long as it recognizes this limitation and stays consistently within it one can have no quarrel with its exponents.

A similar stress upon the positive aspect is characteristic also of *philosophical* reasoning, if we neglect for the moment an exception to be noticed later. The self-imposed limitation in this case springs from the tendency of philosophical, particularly ethical, reasoners to identify *value* with *valuable*, or desirable, and to assume, when not explicitly affirming, that all values are good. This attitude, where not openly expressed in systematic expositions, is often implied in conversations and leads to mutual misunderstanding in academic forums where philosophers and sociologists fraternize. A highly competent philosopher frankly admitted to the writer that he finds the sociological duality quite distasteful to his thought and prefers to use the two terms "values" and "dis-values." This reduces the question to one of terminology and taste, and concerning the matter as thus stated there can be no dispute. However, philosophers who use these two terms, or equivalents, would seem implicitly to recognize that dual aspect of values which has led sociologists to define them as both positive and negative, attractive and repellent. Nevertheless, it is probably correct to say that the majority of philosophers still use the words "value" and "good" as equivalent terms.

While it is no part of the present purpose to attempt a historical survey of the practice of philosophers in this matter, we may permissibly set down in passing a few casual observations. For instance, one notes that the eminent

Danish philosopher, Harald Höffding, in the translation of his *Problems of Philosophy* "arranged for" by William James, assumes that the "problem of values" is comprised in the twofold aspect of "the ethical problem" and "the religious problem." In this tacit manner he identifies values with the search for "a single primordial value that determines the values of single instants, periods of life, abilities, and impulses."[2] Yet this limitation closely follows a sentence wherein he remarks that "whatever conduces to satisfaction or supplies a need has worth, or is a good."[3] Five years later, in 1910, the standard *History of Philosophy* by W. Windelband appeared. This great authority ends his impressive survey with a section entitled "The Problem of Values." At the outset this is taken to be a matter of "ethical considerations," and the position thus tacitly assumed is maintained to the last page.

In like manner a well-developed symposium on "The Arbitrary as Basis for Rational Morality" by C. M. Perry and six collaborators identifies general theory of value with moral value throughout the discussion. It is not unfair to say that we have here the traditional philosophical practice wherein value is identified with good, and particularly with the higher spiritual good. The symposium referred to appeared in the *International Journal of Ethics* in 1933, but the present writer has observed the same identification process in an authoritative college textbook on the history of philosophy, which has appeared since that date. In fact, very recent discussions in private conversation and before two learned societies have found professional philosophers inclined, but not unanimously so, to make use of the term values to indicate only desirable and valuable goals or goods.

If this identification of value with good be essential to the preservation of human faith in the supreme importance of moral and religious values, not to mention those of science and the fine arts, the present writer would be among the first to support that traditional philosophic way of thinking and speaking. But such does not seem to be the case. Even those most zealous to preserve the objectivity and

---

[2]Harald Höffding, *The Problems of Philosophy* (New York, 1905), p. 158.
[3]*Ibid.*, p. 154.

authority of the higher values will recognize that in the realm of morals we have vice as well as virtue, and that religion itself deals with both sin and righteousness, unbelief and faith. Yet in making these admissions, one seems to concede that on every level values are responded to in action as either positive or negative, regardless of any theory on the subject. If there are any serious metaphysical commitments or implications in the positive-negative account now widely prevailing among sociologists, such implications as a professional philosopher would discern, it is much to be desired that such thinkers should be diligent to point them out. Even if sociologists are free from metaphysical blundering in their growing use of this essentially philosophical value concept, it does, nevertheless, seem unfortunate that the exponents of two disciplines so closely related at certain points should be using the important term value in such divergent ways. Agreement in the definition and use of the term is highly desirable from the point of view of the present writer.

Yet while the divergence is regrettable and even disconcerting, it is hard to resolve. The etymology of the word value is apparently on the side of the philosophical usage. We are told that value means, in the original Latin verb, "to be strong, to be worth." This original meaning remains in the German word *Wert*, signifying "value." So, to speak of negative worth (as in the sociologist's phrase "negative value") seems to be a contradiction in terms. One can think of no worth, or worthlessness, but hardly of worthless worth (negative values), if one holds to the original sense of the word. However, if we refuse to be bound too closely by language roots and take "worth" as practically equivalent to "meaning" or "significance," the difficulty vanishes. This is apparently what sociologists, and some philosophers, have done, as will appear in the pages that follow. If the divergence in the use of the word cannot now be undone, perhaps it can be explained, and the fitness or unfitness of the sociological terminology to express the facts of life more closely examined.

However, in making this comparison we have outrun our story, for sociologists have not always occupied their present position. Perhaps it was first taken by Thomas and Znaniecki, in the well-known "Methodological Note," prefacing their celebrated *Polish Peasant* monograph. While the passage in question is not explicit on this point, their definition for a "social value" is "any datum having an empirical content accessible to the members of some social group and a meaning with regard to which it is or may be an object of activity."[4] Reducing this to a brief shorthand expression, we shall here refer to social values as simply *meaningful group objects,* since they are objects having a common meaning for the members of a group. The said meaning is the outcome of group experience. It is evident that neither the experience nor the meaning need be good or desirable. In fact, both may be bad and quite odious without becoming thereby any less truly meaningful group objects, or values, as defined.

In that great monograph, Professors Thomas and Znaniecki were not interested, it seems, in formal definitions, and merely defined these concepts as working mental tools for a specific piece of research. Moreover, they were dealing with *social* values exclusively. Therefore, they did not raise the issue of negative values explicitly. However, in the well-known passage defining a social value they named only positive, or desirable, values in these words, "Thus, a food-stuff, an instrument, a coin, a piece of poetry, a university, a myth, a scientific theory, are social values."[5] The passage leaves room, however, for the positive and negative aspects in a complementary definition of an *attitude,* as "a process of individual consciousness which determines real or possible activity of the individual in the social world."[6] In this statement the "activity" may be conceived as either favorable or hostile, as Professor Thomas clearly assumes in a later writing wherein he said, "there are also negative values—things which exist but which the individual does not want, which he may even despise."[7] Professors Park

---

[4]W. I. Thomas and Florian Znaniecki, *The Polish Peasant in Europe and America* (Chicago, 1918 and 1921), Vol. I, p. 15.

[5]*Ibid.,* p. 21.

[6]*Ibid.,* p. 22.

[7]In *Suggestions of Modern Science Concerning Education,* by Jennings, Thomas, and others (New York, 1917); quoted by Robert E. Park and Ernest W. Burgess in *Introduction to the Science of Sociology* (Chicago, 1921), p. 488.

and Burgess, pushing the same line of analysis further, pointed out that "the two most elementary patterns are the tendency to approach and the tendency to withdraw."[8]

In the brief passages quoted, these three writers thus enunciated the now current sociological doctrine that approach and withdrawal attitudes define positive and negative social values, respectively. Professor Reuter added a suggestive touch when he said: "An object, whether the contact be sensual or imaginary, may be an object of desire to one group, an object of aversion to a second, and to a third remain indifferent—that is, be not a value at all."[9]

In this and similar passages from other sociological writings, one finds the position clearly taken that values are both positive and negative, and neither exclusively good nor bad in their essence as values. That depends upon the actual content of the specific personal, social, or cosmic situation.

We now turn to that step in philosophy which was ignored for the moment in the preceding account. It was taken simultaneously, it seems, by Professor Wilbur Marshall Urban, of Smith College, in his pioneer volume entitled *Valuation: Its Nature and Laws,* published in 1909, and by Professor Ralph Barton Perry in his vigorous little book, *The Moral Economy,* published in the same year. Professor Urban, in his work, the subtitle of which was "An Introduction to the General Theory of Value," gave American philosophy a new picture of the nature of values and valuation in general, although he did not discuss the question of negative values. Professor Perry, in his monograph, laid down premises which were elaborated two decades later in his systematic presentation, *The General Theory of Value.*[10] In *The Moral Economy* Perry's basic proposition, for what later was to develop into a general theory of value, was that a world without life would be a world without good or bad, "a waste of moral indifference." In our present terminology it would be a world without values. Defining an "interest" as any unit of life which strives constantly

---

[8]*Ibid.,* p. 439.

[9]Quoted by Emory S. Bogardus in *Contemporary Sociology* (Los Angeles, 1931), p. 173.

[10]Ralph Barton Perry, *The General Theory of Value* (New York, 1926).

to bring itself to maturity, maintain and perpetuate itself, Professor Perry showed how the appearance of such a living thing, even the tiniest mote, would split the indifferent universe of the inert nonliving into two realms. One of these would be all those aspects of environment which were good for the minute unit of life; the other would be all those which were bad for it. As he observed, this dichotomy of the "good-for" and the "bad-for" sets the stage for the moral drama, which, however, begins only when a second "interest" or life unit appears on the scene. That drama it is not our purpose to consider here, but to call attention to the fact that the moral "stage" of good-for and bad-for described by Professor Perry really also introduced the world of values, in the universal sense.

Perry's interest at that time seemed to lie in setting forth an empirical system of ethics, and he did not expand the implications for a general theory of value until many years later, as shown above.

It is easy to see how from these premises there eventually emerged the definition of a value, in most universal terms, as "any object of any interest," as it appears on page 115 of Perry's *General Theory of Value*. On a later page he says, "That which is an object of interest is *eo ipso* invested with value." (p. 137)

Meanwhile, the present writer, building on the premises laid down by Perry in his earlier book and in his classes at Harvard University, but not yet acquainted with his later work or the early book by Urban, had reached similar conclusions and had framed the definitive proposition that *values are the selected objects of living things*. It will be recognized that this is practically equivalent to Professor Perry's definition as finally formulated. But since it was arrived at independently and has been used by the present writer for several years, it may be permissible to retain it here, with acknowledgments to Professor Perry for the original premise and inspiration.

Several years ago, with the growing conception that values in the generic sense are simply the selected objects of living things, the present writer began a series of seminar studies, with graduate students, into the distinctive meaning of social values. The object was to gain a better grasp of their nature, taking present sociological definitions in their commonly accepted sense. But, as the analysis proceeded, it began to appear that sociologists have been calling many things social values which are not logically in that category. This led to the present effort to state the theory of value in terms of life levels, as will be set forth on the following pages.

It is necessary only to add here that the present statement is the result of a process of elimination, wherein we began with an examination of the term "social values" as currently used in sociology, disclosed the various levels defined below, and were left with a much reduced content for the original term, as is set forth in its proper place on the pages that follow.

Selective behavior of nonliving things. It would be a risky business to wax dogmatic about the difference between the behavior of living things and that of the nonliving. Very evidently the two are essentially different, but the exact nature of the difference is not so clear. To say that living things *select* certain aspects of their environment, while nonliving things do not, very nearly states the situation, if it were not for the selective activities of atoms, molecules, crystals, and colloids. Moreover, all these units manifest *society* in the minimum sense; that is, to a degree which we shall here define as simple *togetherness*. Yet these would seem to be merely striking similarities, or analogies, with the life of the living, and they are accompanied by counterweighting differences. One is that while crystals "grow," they grow by accretion from without and not by metabolic processes from within. Moreover, we know that plants, insects, and even gregarious animals, while living in colonies, swarms, or herds, are really pursuing highly individualistic and solitary lives in spite of their togetherness.[11] Hence, the social life of nonliving entities is very evidently more like our own social life in appearance than it is in fact. Professor Perry rightly began his account of values with the appearance of living things in the hitherto valueless cosmos. In the thought of the present writer,

---

[11]*Cf.* Robert Briffault, "Evolution of Human Species," in *The Making of Man*, by V. F. Calverton, editor (New York, 1931), p. 761 ff., reprinted from *Scientia*, June, 1927.

emergent evolution leaped to a new level with the simulta-
neous arrival of life and values.[12]

Why levels of value arise. We begin at the level of living
organisms, then, in our own attempt to identify and define
the strictly social values, as distinguished from mere aggre-
gations. Living beings are more or less complex organizations of unstable compounds. They are easily hurt or
destroyed. The world around them, organic and inorganic,
is friendly to the individual organism in some ways and
unfriendly to it in others. These positively friendly or unfriendly things stand out from a vast, dim, and undifferentiated background of things that may become either favorable or unfavorable. The primeval mote of Professor Perry
might therefore be said to split the valueless cosmos not only
into the realms of the good-for and bad-for, but also the
what-for—this last being the indifferent, undefined background from which the other two emerge. Every life is
thus a precarious enterprise, a striver biased in its own
favor, bent on its own functioning and perpetuation, in a
world of inanimate matter which apparently does not "care"
for itself, much less for the living beings. Therefore, in
order to live at all, every life unit of whatsoever degree of
simplicity or complexity must take care, and must select
those aspects of the environment which seem good for it or
bad for it. These selected objects of living things are values.
Life is thus the measure of all values, as Robert Briffault
clearly asserted of human beings in his book *The Making
of Humanity.* We do not herein imply, however, that human
life creates all values, but have in mind also subhuman and
superhuman forms of life when we say, with Perry, that
in a world without life there could be no good-for and bad-for,
no good or bad. All values are the selected objects of living
things, approved, rejected, or ignored according to their
bearing upon the drives, purposes, or ideals of the living
beings. There is thus nothing abstruse or vague about the
notion of values in general. It is as simple as an amoeba's

---

[12]See the *Introduction* by Professor Roy W. Sellars to Bouglé's *Evolution of Values* (New York, 1926); also *Emergent Evolution* by C. Lloyd
Morgan [New York, 1922 (1931)], and "Emergent Evolution and Some
of Its Implications," by H. S. Jennings, reprinted from *Science*, Vol. 65,
No. 1672, by the Sociological Press, Hanover, N. H.

doings at one end of the scale, although at the other end particular values may rise to the grandeur of imperishable dreams, immortal hopes, and the divine far-off event toward which the whole creation moves.

In seeking to determine the levels of value we have to keep constantly in mind the basic truth that values are the selected objects of the evaluators themselves. They are not immediately imposed upon the living being, but are selected by it because of its position on the scale of life. More exactly, the values characteristic of each life level are those objects which the being selects by virtue of the fact that it participates with living beings at that level. It may or may not be limited to that particular level in all activities of its being. Consequently, the following named levels are neither mutually exclusive nor all inclusive. Those beings, which alone respond on the higher value levels, at the same time share with humbler beings the values of the lowest levels.

Organic values. Those objects which are sought or avoided by units of life simply because they are organic beings, or living organisms, we shall call organic values. Some such objects selected for avoidance by all organisms are fire and corrosive substances, and heavy, crushing masses. Man and the amoeba are of one mind in this respect because they are both organic beings. They likewise agree in seeking food and drink, air and sunlight, for the same reason. The former group represent negative values of all organisms, the latter are positive values of the same.

Specific values. Specific values are those selected objects which are singled out as favorable or unfavorable by the organism because of the fact that it is a member of a particular species. In other words, specific values are the selected objects of the species. Since each species of plant or animal inherits a distinctive organic structure and specific tropisms, reflexes, instincts, or drives of some sort, it naturally seeks and avoids different things from those attended to by a different species. As organisms they select the same objects; as species they select divergent objects. Hence, as organisms they compete through *commensalism,* while as species they cooperate by means of *mutualism,* like the partnership between the Honey Badger and the Majumba Bird.[13]

Examples of the above are countless in the world of living beings, as the reader well knows. A hen's bodily structure is characterized by a sharp-keeled chest and long, centrally dangling legs ending in slim claws. Consequently, a pond of water offers no attractions for her and is, indeed, a negative value, one to be withdrawn from in precipitation. The duck, on the contrary, with her broad breast and short web-footed legs attached at the rear finds the pond a positive value, to be joyfully approached. Another contrast is seen in the different evaluations placed on bright sunlight by the soaring eagle and the burrowing mole. . . . .

It is well known that among both ants and bees the division of labor is found between those of similar form as well as among the polymorphic subdivisions. Consequently, the selected objects, or values, whether pollen, wax, or nectar, or leaves, chopped leaves, minced leaves, door opening, or what not, are preferred for functional as well as structural reasons within the species; while the structural alone accounts for the divergence in values between these insects and related forms, such as butterflies, beetles, or grasshoppers. One and the same universe presents very different fields of values to a student poring over his books, a tiny gnat poised on a sunbeam beside him, and a fly that looks upon the scene through six eye facets while she crawls upside down along the ceiling overhead.

Social values. It needs to be recalled at this point that the basic fact in all our reasoning here is the preferential behavior of the living things themselves. The structure and attitudes of the evaluators define the values on both the levels already described. More than that, we have seen that the necessarily selective behavior of living things is the measure of all values, although not their creator, as far as we can discern them. This being true, we dare not abandon our method of approach when we come now to consider social values, nor may we do so on any of the other levels of value yet to be defined. The entire pyramid, if we may

---

[13]Don H. Selchow, "A Strange Partnership," *Natural History*, 35:431-37, December, 1935.

so liken it, must rest on the same base and possess the symmetry of self-consistent, logical reasoning—and that requires that we continue to approach on each new level from the point of view of the evaluating beings themselves at that level.

This obvious principle need not have been elaborated were it not for the fact that we are forced at this point to define social values with a narrower connotation than is now the practice among American sociologists; and this we have to do for the following reasons.

Upon the present level of social values, we consider *organisms that live in groups.* This, of course, is not true of all living beings. The honeybee lives in highly organized communities, but the bumblebee roams solitary, as do spiders and many insects. Wasps are much more solitary than bees or ants, but have been known to utilize the same corridor for their ruggedly individualistic family dwellings. Lions loaf in pairs, or in small groups of pairs, with their offspring. Grazing and browsing animals, such as cattle, bison, caribou, and antelopes, go in vast herds, wherein individual animals, or mother and young, live individualistically, each following his own nose for grass or leaves, in a multitudinous solitude analogous to that which some have ascribed to the great city.

Now, if we succeed in identifying strictly social values, they will consist of the objects selected by living things not only because they are organisms, or merely because they are organisms of a certain species, but because they live in groups of two or more. In short, social values are the objects selected by social beings because of the fact that they are social beings. The natural object changes from the merely natural thing to a social value at the point where two or more individuals agree, no matter how tacitly or automatically, upon its meaning. Let us now attempt some examples on this, the social level:

(1) One of these essentially social values is the physical presence of the *associates,* or *socii.* A cow will range for miles in pursuit of grass without paying the least attention to the rest of the herd as long as they are within sight, sound, or smell. But if she wanders inadvertently down a glade, and finally awakens to the fact that the herd has disappeared, her

distress is great, as manifested in frantic bawling and rushing around. When she regains the herd, she may, if sufficiently upset, force her way into its midst in order to get the physical "feel" of the associates against her body.

(2) Implied in the above is a second social value, namely, the herd, flock, or *group* in itself.

(3) A third object, favorably selected or sought by social beings, is recognized position, or *status,* in the group. The writer has more than once observed the struggle for status, a goring order and the enforcement of it, among domestic cattle, while the so-called "pecking order" among fowls is the same thing. Similar behavior among other species shows that social animals select social position as a distinct social value.[14] And, as every sociologist now knows, most of the time and energy of human beings is spent in the gaining, maintaining, and improving of one's social status.

(4) The *group habitat* may be named as a fourth social value in the strict sense as here defined. Social beings select with peculiar interest the beehive, anthill, or home town as a positive value to be sought, and that of another group as a negative one to be avoided, disparaged, or assailed. At least this is true of the social insects, and it is often true of ignorant, untraveled men.

(5) Perhaps *mutual aid* is a social value also. Kropotkin showed with a great array of evidence that the apparently "happier" life of social animals rests upon their recent practice of this kind of behavior. The fact that they select such patterns suggests that it is for them an "interest," as Perry would say it, satisfying a basic "fifth wish," as Bogardus puts it; a positive value in our present phraseology. Whatever the case among animals, we know that mutual aid is a positive social value among human beings in every state of cultural development.

(6) Among human associates, eating and drinking together, or *the common meal,* is a clearly recognized social value of the positive type. It may be an object selected favorably by subhumans also, although one thinks of more instances where it leads to growlings, gorings, clawings, and other

---

[14]Herbert Spencer's chapter on "Ceremonial Societies" in his *Principles of Sociology* (New York, 1909).

combative table manners that mark the common meal as a negative value on the organic level.

(7) With the exception of the last named, all the above social values are positive. *Solitude*, on the other hand, may be mentioned as a negative social value for herd members, perhaps for social insects, and certainly for the vast majority of human beings.

Social-cultural values. Social-cultural values are the selected objects of the members of groups or societies possessing a culture. This is a mode of life that is limited to human beings, in the opinion of most social scientists, although there has been some able and vigorous dissent. That question was discussed with the present writer by Hart, Pantzer, and Bain in earlier issues of the *American Journal of Sociology*, and it need not be reargued here.[15] Just now we must attempt some brief statement of the essential characteristics of culture, in order to define, or at least illustrate, cultural values more clearly. Ward laid a firm foundation when he explained civilization (culture in our phraseology) as the sum total of achievement, and achievement as ways and means of modifying environment by tools and symbols, the knowledge of which is transmitted purely by tradition, especially through the process of democratic education.[16]

This is just about the sum of the matter, yet Ellwood and others improved it by setting forth very ably and explicitly the great role of *language* in the organization and transmission of culture;[17] while Bernard contributed some extremely illuminating ideas when he referred to "the external storage of internal habit systems," and spoke of this as "symbolic behavior."[18] The preceding, with the addition of Wissler's "Universal Culture Scheme" (speech, material traits, art, mythology and scientific knowledge, religious practices, family

[15]*American Journal of Sociology*, 30:703-9, May, 1925, and 32:906-20, May, 1927; also *Sociology and Social Research*, 13: 545-56, July-August, 1929.

[16]Lester F. Ward, *Pure Sociology* (New York and London, 1883), Chap. III; *Applied Sociology* (Boston, 1906), Chap. XII.

[17]Charles A. Ellwood, "Theories of Cultural Evolution," *American Journal of Sociology*, 23:779-800, May, 1918.

[18]L. L. Bernard, "The Classification of Culture," *Sociology and Social Research*, 15:209-29, January-February, 1931.

and social systems, property, government, and war),[19] gives a rather definite notion as to what we here mean by the term "culture."

As defined for the purpose of the present paper, culture is whatsoever man (or any other creature) learns as a member of society, stores externally in tools and symbols, and transmits socially as culture patterns, in their twofold aspect of social values, with corresponding attitudes in persons, plus such products as endure through "the sheer objective continuity of material existence."[20] Cultural values are the objects which living social beings select to seek or avoid, not merely because they are social but because they are members of a group that possesses an accumulating stream of socially transmitted symbolic behavior, as above described.

This kind of behavior is shown by the available evidence to hold only for human beings, with some fragmentary and shadowy suggestions among insects, spiders, and apes. Therefore, our discussion of the present level, and also the next one, may be understood as referring specifically to human beings, the present writer's investigations of a rather large body of evidence having shown that the fact proves insufficient to warrant its extension.

The first fact to arrest attention here is that it is in his cultural life rather than his social traits that man is more richly equipped than are subhuman creatures. This holds true, apparently, for both community organization and individual social traits. As for organization, we see that in the elaborate societies of ants and bees man is rivaled if not outdone. Indeed the present drift toward regimentation in dictatorial nations today has been interpreted explicitly by some as a movement toward the life plan of the social insects. Of one thing we may be certain, namely, that in the ruthless regimentation of the anthill and beehive we see a perfect model for the so-called "efficient," "totalitarian" society.

When it comes to certain basic social attitudes, the behavior of the subhuman creatures is amazing in many instances. The self-sacrificing affection of the mother for her offspring loses nothing as we descend the scale of mammalian life, as every

---

[19]Clark Wissler, *Man and Culture* (New York, 1923), chaps. IV and V.
[20]*Cf.* A. F. Goldenweiser, *Early Civilization* (New York, 1922), p. 17 for the quoted phrase.

observer of domestic animals knows.   The affection of the little chimpanzee, Gua, that Professor and Mrs. Kellogg experimentally "adopted" and treated exactly as they did their infant son, Donald, could hardly be counted as less than human in its warmth and definiteness of affectionate expression toward its little human playmate.[21]

This same young ape also expressed most remarkably definite attitudes of approach and withdrawal, or social distance, with reference to different persons who had shown various degrees of sympathy, understanding, and tactful bearing in their dealings with it.   This expression varied from a long, warm handclasp to a hesitating approach and a greeting so brief that it amounted merely to a quick slap of the palm and a swift leap backward at the same instant.   This fine social intelligence was not matched by cultural facility, since, as the experimenters say, she was *only an ape* in the end.

The fascinating account of beaver traits given by the Indian ex-trapper and warden, Grey Owl, in his book, *Pilgrims of the Wild*,[22] shows these creatures as being extraordinarily "human" in their affection for one another and also for Grey Owl and his Iroquois wife.   All this, and much additional evidence, is sufficient to show that in strictly social traits mankind does not rate so much beyond the so-called brutes as is often assumed.   His superiority lies in his cultural rather than in his social development.

However, the distinction between the social and the cultural is not clearly discernible at this point, particularly when we pause to consider the origin of the thing which is called "human nature."   Its leading expositor, Professor Cooley, described it as

a social nature developed in man by simple forms of intimate association or "primary groups," especially the family and neighborhood, which are found everywhere and everywhere work upon the individual in somewhat the same way.   This nature consists chiefly of certain primary social sentiments and attitudes, such as consciousness of one's self in relation to others, love of approbation, resentment of censure, emula-

[21]Winthrop Niles Kellogg and Luella Kellogg, *The Ape and the Child: A Study of Environmental Influence upon Early Behavior* (New York, 1933).

[22]Wa-Sha-Quon-Asin (Grey Owl), *Pilgrims of the Wild* (New York, 1935).

tion, and a sense of social right and wrong formed by the standards of a group.[23]

These traits, particularly the last two, are distinctively human. Professor Cooley so regarded them, as shown by the fact that he spoke of these human nature sentiments and impulses as human "in being superior to those of lower animals," yet "not something existing separately in the individual, but a *group-nature or primary phase of society*. . . . Man does not have it by birth; he cannot acquire it except through fellowship, and it decays in isolation . . . the family and neighborhood life is essential to its genesis and nothing more is."[24] Thus, it seems that human nature as defined by Cooley turns out to be not only social but cultural, and man's superiority in social traits, whatever its degree, is tied up inextricably with his cultural experience.

In view of the above and other considerations already mentioned, the second thing to be noted in the present discussion is that the values which recent sociology has been calling "social" are often really cultural values. That is to say, an instrument, a coin, a piece of poetry, a university, a myth, a scientific theory are all things that man has learned as a member of society. The only remaining one of this famous list of examples from Thomas and Znaniecki is foodstuffs. They may include a simple organic value such as a meaty bone, a strictly social value such as the queen's honey or jelly fed by her bodyguard to a queen bee, or a cultural value such as "Mellin's Food." The other objects in the above list all imply conceptual or symbolic thinking, which is really abstract thinking and particular to mankind, so far as we know. We do know, at any rate, that animals have no coins, universities, myths, or theories.

At the same time we do not overlook the fact, acknowledged where we spoke of social values as meaningful group objects, that all cultural objects are the outcome of social or group experience, as Professor Thomas so clearly showed. Therefore, it might be better to speak of such collectively selected and meaningful group objects as social-cultural values. We should then have the strictly social values named in the pre-

---

[23]Cooley, *Human Nature and the Social Order* (New York, 1902; revised edition, 1922), p. 32.
[24]Cooley, *Social Organization* (New York, 1909), pp. 28, 29, 30-31.

ceding section and common to man and subhuman social cultures, and the social-cultural values peculiar to man.

Social-cultural values are likewise the only ones, naturally, named by Wissler in his "universal culture scheme." The list is, as he states, merely suggestive and schematic. The number of social-cultural values is beyond enumeration. Even the gigantic catalogue of a great mail-order house represents only part of the wealth of material objects known to occidental culture, and material objects make up only one ninth of Wissler's culture scheme. Against this bewildering multiplicity of social-cultural values stands the list of seven strictly social values as already presented. . . . .

Personal values. Personal values are the objects selected by a person as such, that is as an individual who has integrated his own experiences and acquired his social status, high or low, within certain culture groups. The word *person* means to us two things. First, the person, as personality, is the spiritual self of Eubank.[25] So regarded, it is that unfathomed entity which holds memories and formulates purposes. It is the integrating center of all the experiences of the individual. In the suggestive phrase of Korzybski and his associates, it is the "time-binder." For the present writer this signifies the living thing *for which time counts* by registering impressions, and funding them as attitudes and habits. As a time binder it thus picks up its own past and carries it within itself through the present into the future. In so doing this time binder, memory holder, experience haver, status seeker, ideal cherisher remains always the same, yet forever changing—a paradox which only personality can resolve, as Professors Borden P. Bowne and Ralph T. Flewelling have shown.[26] In so doing, it comes to select certain objects just because of its own private experience in the past. Thus one person may enjoy pleasant recollections when certain musical strains are played because so conditioned to them by a happy experience of the distant school days, and it is therefore a positive value for him. Another may respond in precisely the opposite way as a result of an unpleasant setting in his

---

[25]Earle Edward Eubank, *The Concepts of Sociology* (New York, 1932), pp. 103-6.

[26]Ralph Tyler Flewelling, *Personalism and the Problems of Philosophy* (New York, 1915), pp. 134-35 and 184.

past for the same strains, making it for him a negative value. Both life and literature are full of illustrations of this power of private, unique experience to create a set of personal values.

At the same time, the person is an individual who has attained recognized position, or status, in various groups, large and small. As Eubank ably shows,[27] the person is the "situation self," which varies from situation to situation as the person plays his different roles. Thus the social context is also registered in his approaches and withdrawals with reference to the various objects, material and immaterial. Yet at the same time, as Eubank also shows, the personality, or spiritual self, maintains its identity and integrates the whole stream of experience.

In the light of the above considerations, it seems that personal values fall midway between organic and specific values, both of which are defined by the individual organism, and the social and cultural values, especially the latter, which are determined by the group. Personal values, in other words, are primarily, even uniquely, individual selections, but are socially conditioned in their origin.

This is the proper point to recognize that there are those who are inclined to distinguish a level of individual values. To the present writer it seems, at this time, that individuality is simply that degree of difference, distinctness, or uniqueness which is found among living beings at every level of life. Any creature born with peculiar development, for better or worse, of any organ reacts in a way not quite the same as do its normal companions. This may cause it to select the same objects in a different way, which would be an expression of its individuality but would not create a new level of values. Such variations run throughout the living world, expressing themselves most markedly along both mental and physical lines at the level of human personality. However, in the present thought of the writer, there would seem to be no such thing as a level of individual values. Distinctness, or individual uniqueness, is an aspect of life at every level of values from the lowest to the highest, and values of any level may take on a shade of difference because of this individual characteristic of the evaluator, which is to say, the actor. Moral

---

[27]Eubank, *op. cit.*, pp. 106-10.

and spiritual values are provided for amply, it would seem, under our account of the social-cultural and personal levels of value, without the necessity of introducing a distinct level of "individual" values.

A scale of social-cultural values. Our final level in this account was that of social-cultural values, and, like all other values, they are found to be both positive and negative, that is, good or bad. This duality is in itself sufficient to reassure any reader who might fear that our reasoning will reduce all values to a dead level. On the contrary, we have not even touched a very important remaining problem, perhaps the most important, which is the construction of a scale for rating the multitude of social-cultural values, especially those of the positive, desirable type, which we pronounce good. This, however, may be the special task of philosophy and ethics, if we include social ethics and social philosophy, both of which are highly important, as Simmel so ably showed.[28] All that need be added here is to suggest that a scale might be based upon such characteristics as imperativeness, universality, and inclusiveness—with the addition, of course, of such other criteria as might be found appropriate; for example:

a. Imperativeness. Certain values are absolutely imperative, such as the demand of all organisms for air to breathe, even if it be the air found in the waters where myriads of creatures swim. The Black Hole of Calcutta is the supreme example of this in human history. Next to air come food and drink, to which list other especially imperative values might be added by competent investigators. They would find an excellent body of material and reasoning in the "man-land ratio" of Sumner and Keller.[29] "The first task of life is to live," as Sumner says in his *Folkways*. This does not, of course, imply that it is the highest task, but the most imperative, except with those heroic martyrs who sacrifice life itself to even higher values.

b. Universality. This category overlaps the preceding in one aspect, but is differentiated by the fact that it is here

---

[28]Nicholas J. Spykman, *The Social Theory of Georg Simmel* (Chicago, 1925), Chap. IV.

[29]William G. Sumner and Albert G. Keller, *The Science of Society* (New Haven and London, 1927), Vol. I, Chap. II.

meant to denote also the range of appeal to the possessors of cultural life or, in a word, to mankind. Here the well-known discussion in Cooley's *Social Process* on "human nature values" and "institutional values" affords a fine illustration. The same may be said of the more recent "common-human" and "circumscribed" relations of Von Wiese and Becker's *Systematic Sociology*. Universality of appeal is not exactly the same as imperativeness, since we here deal with things that are not absolutely necessary for the physical existence. However, fair play may be found, in the end, to be equally necessary for the social life. Indeed, before World War I it was apparently so rated, and one of the greatest evils of that conflict was the weakening of regard for fair play and chivalry among millions. And this was not by any means limited to those at the front. It may be that courage still holds its appeal and might be named as another example of a more nearly universal social-cultural value.

c. *Inclusiveness*. Professor Perry did a fine piece of work along this line in *The Moral Economy*. In fact, his table, called "The Order of Virtue," is worked out upon the test of inclusiveness. That is morally better, in his analysis, which more fully preserves and enhances life in a more inclusive way. This is true, he finds, not because it is larger, but because it includes itself, plus other interests of the same kind. Thus, in a conflict of claims between the individual and his family, the family takes precedence, provided it be a true family, since it then includes the interests of all its members, not excepting the one who conflicts in this case. After the same reasoning, the family should yield to the community, provided it be a true community, which then includes the welfare of that particular family plus that of all the other families. And so on, upward through the commonwealth, nation, and internation, or humanity at large. On Perry's scale, religion stands at the top, as it should, because its "value" is "the universal system of interests," realized through the virtue called "good-will." Durkheim's division of all values into the secular and the sacred[30] supports this view; and, likewise, Lowie's dichotomy of the "ordinary" and the "extraordinary."

---

[30] Emile Durkheim, *The Elementary Forms of the Religious Life* (London and New York, 1915); Robert H. Lowie, *Primitive Religion* (New York, 1924).

Still earlier, King, in his penetrating study, *The Development of Religion,* showed clearly that religious values are necessarily, for psychological reasons, the most transcendent values.[31] Indeed, if religion did not fill this role, it would not be religion, which is precisely the organization of the higher values of any social-cultural group, or man's completest response to his biggest world. And, as shown above, the religious values are "higher" because, for one thing, they are more inclusive, in the temporal as well as the spatial dimensions. Professor Urban, in his article on "value" in the *Encyclopaedia Britannica,* writes as follows in raising the question of an ultimate standard of values:

> In general such a standard is found in the notion of *inclusiveness,* in some functional conception such as the totality of life or experience, that value being highest which contributes most to the coherent functioning and organization of experience as a whole. Such a standard may be formulated in terms that seem to avoid metaphysical implications, but in general it may be said that the highness or lowness of an experience of value is held to be determined by its metaphysical content. From this point of view a very common table or scale of values is that which puts the economic values as the lowest and the religious (in the broadest sense) as the highest, the ethical, the logical, and the aesthetic being arranged in various ways in between.

The ancient division of the higher social-cultural values into the three categories of the *true,* the *beautiful,* and the *good* has been approved by numerous modern thinkers as perhaps most satisfactory, and some very properly include as a fourth, the *useful.*

Upon this basis we should then have the useful in the three aspects of the most imperative, the most universal, and the most inclusive, making likewise this threefold differentiation under each of the other three categories. Finally, there should be mentioned Dean Small's "health, wealth, sociability, knowledge, beauty, and rightness." In this there is an expansion of the four categories named above, under a twofold progression, namely, from the more egoistic to the more altruistic, and from the more material values to the more spiritual.*

---

[31]Irving King, *The Development of Religion: A Study in Anthropology and Social Psychology* (New York, 1910), chaps. IV and V, *et passim.*

*Reprinted from *Sociology and Social Research,* 23:403-30, May-June, 1939.

CONFLICT AND COOPERATION IN SOCIAL PROGRESS*

THE RELATION between conflict and cooperation presents one of the most fundamental and far-reaching problems of sociology, usually discussed hitherto by sociologists with rather exclusive emphasis on one or the other of its aspects.[1] On the whole, it might be said that the conflict theorists had the first word in sociological thinking, and the notion of the importance of conflict, even including war, dominated sociological theory for many years. The leaders in this field of thought were Gumplowicz and Ratzenhofer, both of them natives of central Europe, where a turmoil of nations, loosely held together under successive conquests, made conflict appear to be the principal social process. The teaching of these Austrians was adopted by Lester F. Ward and got its hold in American sociological thinking in consequence of his very great influence in that field. Sumner also supported the same idea in his *War and Other Essays,* while Giddings is not entirely free from emphasizing it in the concluding essay of his *Democracy and Empire*—this chapter being entitled "The Gospel of Non-Resistance."

Farther back this whole line of thought rests upon a somewhat gross misinterpretation and false emphasis which was placed by biologists first, and later by social thinkers, upon certain aspects of the Darwinian theory of evolution. According to this misinterpretation of that theory the fundamental law of life is one of individual struggle not only by members of different species but also by members of the same species. This has been taught by biologists for decades, in their loose utterances if not on their definite intention, and has come to be part of the everyday philosophy of multitudes. This philosophy is summed up in the saying "Dog eat dog," which is commonly used to justify all kinds of aggression and oppression in social and international life. The fact is, however, that this is a gross misinterpretation

---

*Remarks at the California State Conference for Social Work, May, 1924.

[1]Emory S. Bogardus, *A History of Social Thought* (Los Angeles, 1922). The principal contributions from both sides will be found summed up in Chap. XX, "Conflict Theories in Sociology," and Chap. XXI, "Cooperation Theories in Sociology."

of the facts of nature. Dog never eats dog, and lion does not eat lion; neither does tiger eat tiger. The only creature foracious enough to kill members of his own species is man himself. He has sunk so low at times as actually to devour bodies of his fellow humans, under what we know as cannibalism. Later this was softened into slavery, by which system the master eats his slave many times over in the course of his lifetime, by devouring his product and by sometimes working him to death. In modern times slavery has been softened, first into wage slavery and more recently into profiteering in all its luxuriant developments.

Nothing of this kind, however, takes place among animals of the same species, as has been shown with tremendous array of evidence by so distinguished a naturalist and sociologist as Prince Kropotkin in his notable work *Mutual Aid*. According to Kropotkin the members of no animal species prey upon one another, but constantly support and assist one another by many most marvelous devices and arrangements for cooperation or, as he calls it, "mutual aid." It is therefore a gross libel to speak of man as falling to the level of the brute. Far from falling to the level of the brute, it would be necessary for human beings who destroy and devour one another to reach up in order to touch bottom, for they are far below the level of the brute in such matters. It is taken as evidence of scandalous ferocity of temper when one hears it remarked among us that somebody fell to the level of a brute, but it must be a much more scandalous thing among animals to hear it whispered that one of them fell to the level of a human. . . . . .

The current social philosophy which justifies war upon the notion that it is simply an expression of the universal struggle for existence indicated by Darwin is utterly and hopelessly false, without the slightest foundation in the facts of animal life — much more without any foundation in ethics or truly human ideals. As a corollary, the sociology of war and conflict which ran current up to the time of World War I is practically worthless; and, since there is a vast deal of it, our sociological shelves will be happily unburdened when the mass of it is recognized as fit only for the rubbish heap. The fundamental error in it consists in the assumption cited above and the further fact that most thinkers among social scientists in all fields have overlooked the truth which is now forcing itself upon us, namely, that war has completely changed its character since 1914. That is to say, it has become so destructive that none of the things that were said about war before that time would hold true concerning the institution in its new aspects. We read of Richard the Lionhearted carrying twenty pounds of steel in his battle axe, and we have been entertained by the stories of the exploits of the knights of old on a thousand battlefields, but we have overlooked the fact that they stood up all afternoon, or rode around on horseback, securely clad in something resembling a modern kitchen range, and battered each other until sunset without doing much more damage than a lively football game in the early days of that modern sport. In other words, those combats were comparatively harmless, while with modern methods of slaughter, such as will be used in the next war undoubtedly, more people, including women and children as well as men, and civilians at that, will be slain in thirty minutes than were destroyed during all the combats of the entire Middle Ages. In the face of these facts the prattle about war as an expression of the universal law of life is grotesque.

But, while many sociologists have fallen into this false line of thought, there have not been lacking those who perceive the futility of such reasoning. We have already mentioned Kropotkin; and the names of Ross, Ellwood, Novicow, Small, Cooley, Hobhouse, and others should be mentioned. These writers have stressed a truth equally great, namely, that cooperation is a fundamental process of all life, particularly human life. Professor Cooley, in his analysis of this subject, as in all his writings, is especially penetrating. He says: "It is possible rudely to classify hostilities in three parts, according to the degree of mental organization they involve." "These are as follows: (1) primary, immediate, or animal; (2) social, imaginative, or personal of a comparatively direct sort, that is, without reference to any standard of justice; (3) rational or ethical; similar to the last but involving reference to a standard of justice and the sanction of conscience."[2]

---

[2]Charles H. Cooley, *Human Nature and the Social Order* (New York, 1902), p. 239.

The problem of personal and social advancement is to raise hostility from the lower to the higher level so that it will express itself less and less in the personal or brutal forms and take on more that of the rational or ethical. We need not hope to see perfect harmony and unanimity attained in society. In fact, we should not desire this. It would be hard to imagine anything more deadly dull than to live in a world where one had to agree with everybody else. Disagreement is fundamental for the attainment of a higher potentiality of thought and action. Conflict also has its permanent place in human affairs. The only question is how to refine and turn it toward constructive ends by constructive methods. As sociologists have pointed out, it is possible for one to live in any group only because of the fact that one retains the right of criticism and protest, or of disagreement in some form or other. There are many groups which would be blown to pieces by an explosion of repressed emotion and passion, if for a sufficient length of time unanimity of action were enforced, so that one should find no means of registering his dissent, and if at the same time he were prevented from withdrawal. It is only by means of withdrawal—either actually, i. e., physically, or by a kind of nonphysical withdrawal, in which one simply maintains no social contacts with the offending persons or groups— that life becomes endurable at all in certain situations. One can live in a big city, for example, along with people following practices and standards one may utterly detest, simply because one maintains the right of dissenting from their ways or views in word or in deed, either passively or actively. The way, then, to maintain social life upon a basis of disagreement and conflict is to provide more and different forms of expression and a wider range of action, so that the individual may choose his own associates and alliances, and through these alliances, or in person, come into conflict and struggle with other persons and groups, opposing vigorously but not destructively; or, in other words, lift conflict from the merely physical to the social, rational, and ethical levels. It is only under such circumstances that society can function on the highest level of potentiality.

Now, a word about noncooperation. When one studies the movement led by Mahatma Gandhi in India and similar movements in history, both current and ancient, notably the boycott of American merchants against British tea and other goods in Revolutionary times, one comes to realize the tremendous social importance of noncooperation under certain circumstances. Gandhi—barefoot and barehanded, a humble, poorly clad ascetic, the meekest of mortals in his personal behavior—recently led the millions of his Indian fellow citizens in a noncooperative protest against British domination which nearly overthrew the Empire in India. A great sociological truth may be learned from this movement, and that is that the fundamental law of life is, after all, cooperation, so fundamental that every form of exploitation and tyranny requires for its continued existence the tacit cooperation of even the victims themselves. When the victims cease to cooperate the oppressors must fall. So, after all, the fundamental thing is cooperation and organization.

This leads to another process, which Sumner called antagonistic cooperation, such as that between employer and employee, between teacher and pupil, and in the domestic circle, as typified by the cartoonist in the well-known story of Andy Gump and Min. In all such cases there is a more or less superficial antagonism, mutual criticism, or other form of conflict, which rests upon a still more fundamental community of interest and unity of purpose. Examination of the law of society will reveal the fact that a vast deal of our harmonious existence is in forms of the antagonistic cooperation just described.

War, the most destructive form of conflict, will have to be eliminated by the application of both noncooperation and cooperation. The more negative method is exemplified in the agreement of the International Metal Workers to refuse to make or handle munitions in the event of a declaration of war; in the proposed resolutions by which the churches would withdraw their support from all war; and in the extraordinary Non-Cooperation movement led by Gandhi in India. Beyond this, it may prove necessary for the masses in all lands to form a World Peace Union, pledging themselves to paralyze war by refusing to take part in it, not to cooperate with it in any way. This would be a drastic measure, made necessary only by the blind persistence of small-minded politicians, who perpetuate an evil tradition among nations in the interest, consciously or unconsciously, of profiteers in all lands.

But beyond these temporary, negative measures lies the great task of promoting cooperation among the nations in positive ways. This means a World Court, a World League, and a determined policy of working together along economic and cultural lines. By cooperating, which literally means "working together," the nations will come to understand one another, and that will mark the end of race prejudice, hostility, and war.

Prince Kropotkin, in his great work, *Mutual Aid*, anticipated our most recent thought on this problem of international organization when he said: "In the practice of mutual aid, which we can trace to the earliest beginnings of evolution, we thus find the positive and undoubted origin of our ethical conceptions; and we can affirm that in the ethical progress of man, mutual support—not mutual struggle—has had the leading part. In its wide extension, even at the present time, we also see the best guarantee of a still loftier evolution of our race."*

*Reprinted from *Journal of Applied Sociology*, 9:179-86, January-February, 1925.

LEADERSHIP AND CONJUNCTURE

A SOCIOLOGICAL HYPOTHESIS

CERTAIN TALK about "teaching leadership," current at times in educational circles, led the writer to question whether there is actually any such thing as leadership traits in general; or anything else sufficiently abstract and universal about leadership to render the *teaching* of it at all possible. In other words, is not leadership simply one fleeting aspect of a changing social or human situation? Does not leadership itself disappear along with other aspects, such as *followership*, as the situation changes? Indeed, was it not just these shifting relations which, taken together, made up the situation itself in its sum and substance? At the outset leadership seemed to be more truly a matter of social situation than of personality traits, but gradually there came into view a third factor, namely, the event. The falling together, or conjuncture, of these three factors produces leadership or, more accurately, the act of leading, according to the hypothesis herein proposed.

The word "conjuncture" was suggested by its use in the field of economics, as may be most briefly shown by the following quotation from Alfred Marshall.

This term is a familiar one in German economics, and meets a need which is much felt in English economics. For "opportunity" and "environment," the only available substitutes for it, are sometimes rather misleading. By *conjunctur*, says Wagner, "we understand the sum total of the technical, economic, social and legal conditions . . . which determine the demand for and supply of goods and therefore their exchange value . . . ."[1]

Paraphrasing this, we see in conjuncture, as used in the present paper, the sum total of the personal, social, and historical conditions that determine the demand for and the supply of leadership in human interaction. The three factors are defined as follows for the purpose of this hypothesis.

Personality traits represent the more abiding aspects of leadership, although they themselves are conceived of as in process of change and development. Among them we may mention those "characteristics of the person which affect his social status and efficiency: (a) physical traits . .;

---

[1] Alfred Marshall, *Principles of Economics* (New York, 1907), p. 125.

(b) temperament; (c) character; (d) social expression . .; (e) prestige . .; (f) the individual's conception of his role." These are so listed by Park and Burgess.[2] To them let us add Floyd H. Allport's "Traits of Personality,"[3] among which appear such rather permanent traits as perceptual ability, emotional breadth, insight, and drive.

The *social situation,* already treated in its relation to leadership by Emory S. Bogardus,[4] was originally defined by Thomas and Znaniecki[5] as involving "three kinds of data." They say:

(1) The objective conditions under which the individual or society has to act, that is, the totality of values—economic, social, religious, intellectual, etc.—which at the given moment affect directly or indirectly the conscious status of the individual or the group. (2) The pre-existing attitudes of the individual or the group which at the given moment have an actual influence upon his behavior. (3) The definition of the situation, that is, the more or less clear conception of the conditions and consciousness of the attitudes.

The person, with his traits, facing a constellation of social values and attitudes in other persons, thus gives us two of our factors. The third is the *event.* At this point we have to point out that these three factors are not mutually exclusive, since the definition of the situation by the person in itself constitutes part of the social situation, but is also included under the individual's conception of his role, which we have accepted above as a personal trait. The same overlapping appears when we consider the event, which seems at first glance to be an aspect of the social situation. This, to be sure, it is, but a quite special aspect. An event is a form of change just as a social situation is a process of many changes in itself. Moreover, the growth of personality is a process of mental integration and disintegration in large part. So it appears that all our factors are aspects or forms of change. Yet this need not disconcert us, since leadership, the very thing we are seeking to factor, is itself a form of change, a process of society, of

[2]*Cf.* Robert E. Park and Ernest W. Burgess, *Introduction to the Science of Sociology* (Chicago, 1921), p. 70.

[3]*Cf.* Floyd H. Allport, *Social Psychology* (Boston, 1924), p. 103.

[4]*Cf.* Emory S. Bogardus, "Leadership and Social Situations," *Sociology and Social Research,* 14:164-70, November-December, 1931.

[5]*Cf.* W. I. Thomas and Florian W. Znaniecki, *The Polish Peasant in Europe and America* (New York, 1927), Vol. I, p. 68.

interaction between the person and his associates, or with the group as a whole.

An *event* is, as historians have always regarded it, a significant or outstanding change. It is part and parcel of the stuff that the world is made of, namely activity and change, but it receives, and deserves, a special name. The reason for this may be shown by the following quotation from Frederick J. Teggart wherein he holds:

> The current acceptance of "events" as important in and for themselves will give place to the concept of events as the active element in change; events will be conceived, not as the expression of the will-acts of individuals, but as "intrusions," of whatever sort, affecting conditions in which the processes manifested in "fixity" have been operative without disturbance. . . .
>
> The identification of "events" as "intrusions" is a matter of some importance. To each an understanding of "how things work" in the course of time, we may envisage the facts of experience as arranged conceptually in a series of concentric circles. Outermost, we would have the stellar universe; within this, the physical earth; within this, the world of organic life; within this, again, the world or organic life; within this, again, the world of human activities; within this, the larger group, or nation; within this, the local community; and finally, within this, the individual. In such a series, it is obvious that change in any outer circle will affect all that lies within it. We may, then, define an "event" as an intrusion, from any wider circle, into any circle or condition which may be the object of present interest.[6]

The sentence last quoted is our ground for regarding, in the present theory of leadership as conjuncture, any intrusive change, no matter how trivial or private, as an event if its disrupts the smooth flow of routinary change, of static, recurrent social process, within the field of interest or leadership under consideration at the moment. For no sociologist needs to be told that leadership of an alley gang is just as valid a case as leadership of the allied nations, although not, of course, so important for human affairs.

The present hypothesis is that the conjuncture, or falling together, of personality traits, social situation, and event determines leadership from hour to hour in the relations of obscure persons, and from time to time in the affairs of the world.*

---

[6]*Cf.* Frederick J. Teggart, *Theory of History* (New Haven, 1925), pp. 148-49.

*Reprinted from *Sociology and Social Research*, 17:510-18, July-August, 1933.

THE CAVE MAN STARTED THIS DEPRESSION*

THIS PAPER is not an attempt at the facetious, but a serious effort to show the workings of a process that began with the first crude tool and ended only with that vast complex of technological and social mechanisms nowadays known as "the machine." The central idea is that we have here a process of *abstraction* in the essential meaning of that term, which has been developed elsewhere by the present writer.[1] In this basic sense, as its roots indicate, the word "abstract" means the action by which one singles out a certain aspect of a concrete whole, and treats it in separation from the whole. Thus, in statistical operations the investigator may "abstract," or draw away, the aspect of age in years from that concrete whole which makes a human personality, and deal with the age factor alone in treating of the population.

The same process is at work in the act of *analyzing* anything whatsoever. For instance, a beaver gnawing down a tree is part and parcel of a concrete, total situation, in which his own role may be played instinctively and largely unconsciously in so far as he has not set himself over against the other factors, namely, the tree and the stream, as a distinct and purposeful factor. The primitive man who uses an axe to fell the tree has, on the contrary, separated the factors, introduced one of his own providing, and, as we shall see, set in motion a process by which he separates himself from the thing on which he is working. For the time being this results in an increase of power and, consequently, of both leisure and output for the worker. Yet, as the technological process has worked itself out in connection with the economic-social process, it has resulted, after centuries and even milleniums, in separating man the worker not only from the materials upon which he works but also from the chance to work at all. The worker always was both a "hand" and a mouth." When the "owners" of the new automatic machines decided to get along with-

---

*This paper was written during the depression of the 1930's.

[1]*Cf.* "Tools and Culture," p. 72; "Machines and Civilization," p. 84; and "Beyond Civilization," p. 120.

out hands, they overlooked the little item of mouths—and also the item of little mouths that the now discarded "hand" still has to fill.

We have here a set of values so absolutely basic that it seems unbelievable that a violent revolution should be required to enable the machine exploiters to recognize them. Yet such has usually been the course of history. In what follows the writer tries to state the case so simply that it might be called the anthropology and sociology of the present world depression in words of one syllable. If it should help to turn from their blind fatuity those who put machines above men and point them toward that peaceful and truly human society that should be ours, the reader may feel disposed to pardon this simple tale.

Tools. Probably the first tool ever used by primitive man was a club torn from a fallen tree or a stone picked up beside the path. In many parts of the earth the ground is strewn with water-worn stones of hard texture, prepared by geological processes to fit the human hand with a smooth, heavy, and convenient aid in cracking nuts, splitting marrowbones, and doing similar tasks. When so used, it may be regarded as a harder, heavier fist. Anthropologists agree in calling such an instrument a "hammerstone." It represents the earliest tools used by man — used but not *made* by him. It was made by nature but *found* and adopted by man. It was used by him to increase the power of his own organs, his fist in this instance, over the physical environment. When he used the club already mentioned, he lengthened his *arm*, as it were. When he split the end of the club and fastened the stone into the cleft with pitch and rawhide thongs, he provided himself with a harder, heavier fist on the end of a longer arm.

This process, so brief in the telling, required a long time, perhaps thousands of years, in the doing. It is commonly so pictured by prehistorians, although it might have happened quite swiftly, and very early in the existence of mankind on this planet. Whatever the date, it was the real beginning of culture, of civilization, and also of the vast unemployment that now baffles the modern world. It came about in the manner described in the pages that follow.

When man placed a hammerstone, and later a stone axe, between himself and the objects which he wished to pound or chop, he separated himself from his work to that extent. The beaver, gnawing directly with his own chisel-like teeth, worked directly on the tree and did a swift and neat piece of work upon it. Primitive man gnawed it down with his stone axe, much more slowly and far less neatly than the beaver could do it. Nevertheless his axe vastly increased the tree-cutting power of man just as soon as he learned to use bronze and iron for its blade. The same increase of power holds true for all tools. Indeed, a tool is anything placed between man and his physical environment to increase the power of his own organs over that environment.

Compound tools. The simple tools just described not only increased man's power over the environment but separated him, at least an arm's length, from that environment. Then he invented the *compound* tool. A good example of this is a pair of pincers, where one part works on the other by means of a pivot. A still better one is the pulley. In this case the human worker pulls on the rope, the rope turns the wheel, and the wheel helps to lift the weight. The wheel itself is a series of levers which automatically take their place in turn as the rope passes through. But the most significant thing about it is that one part moves the other. Thus man, as the prime, or first, mover, was placing himself a step farther from the thing upon which he was working. The step was slight, and really increased his power at the time, but unsuspected mischief was wrapped up in it, to come out only a long time later.

Muscle-driven machines. The next step was to invent the wheel. This is perhaps the greatest invention ever made by mankind, although nobody knows just when and how it was done. At any rate, the wheel made possible not only carts and other vehicles of the kind but also very simple machines such as cornshellers, hand drills, and grindstones, the first on the farm, the second in the blacksmith shop, and the third in both places. Machines of this kind were driven by human muscle. The grindstone was the most simple, being itself a wheel of stone turned directly by means of a crank. The hand drill and cornsheller had a heavy flywheel attached by cogs to the blades or bit, called working parts, and it was designed to keep their motion steady. It also carried the motion over pauses in the muscular effort of the workman, and by its weight and momentum made the working parts more powerful, more steady, and more effective.

After a time at this, probably many generations, men hit on the idea of placing an animal, such as a horse or ox, in a treadmill, and hooking this, by a flywheel and belt, to the machine they wished to use. Scarcely a generation ago horses and treadmills were driving circular saws for cutting cordwood in all parts of the United States. In so doing man lightened his own work, rested his own muscles, and took still another little step toward separating himself from his work in the future.

For the present, however, he found plenty to do in managing the horse, oiling and repairing the machinery, lugging the materials to the machine, and bearing the product away. In short, up to this stage, machinery was an aid, or ally, to the human worker. He usually owned his own tools and simple machines, so that he himself enjoyed the benefits of it. These were the lightening of heavy toil, the shortening of the working day, and the increase of the product of labor.

Power-driven machines. At this stage a new step was taken, by which both human and animal muscular strength was put aside and inanimate natural forces were made to drive the machines. These forces were falling water, blowing winds, and expanding steam. Everywhere in the civilized world of both Occident and Orient appeared the dam and millrace of the old water mill used for sawing lumber and grinding grain. Likewise, the landscape, especially in such countries as the Netherlands of Europe, came to be dotted with windmills, always picturesque, and especially so in the beginning, when they caught the breeze with huge, revolving sails. Equally beautiful to the artistic eye were the water mills, placed not only in every village and city of the river valleys but also high up in the forested hills and mountains where backwoods settlements sat perched around the headwaters of the streams.

This stage in the evolution of civilization, where life was based upon the motive power of wind and water, used wood as its principal material, and was centered in the country and the forest, has been called the Eotechnic period. It was perhaps the most beautiful and truly human stage or epoch in history. . . . .

Capital and power-driven machines. We find that the nations of Europe and America did not show the same caution as those of the ancient East. On the contrary, they rushed pell-mell into what is called the machine economy. This is marked especially by the *factory* system. A factory is simply a building large enough, and properly equipped, to house the new machines, which were given a fresh start by a series of inventions. Notable among these were the spinning wheel, power loom, and steam engine, all either invented or greatly improved by the close of the eighteenth century.

Machines driven by steam engines were more economical when massed in large numbers and driven from the same central drive shaft. This produced a great and sudden change in the relation between the workman, his tools, and his work. For ages he had owned his own kit or chest of the simple hand tools long in use. Even after these were made slightly more complex and driven by wind or water, as above described, men of limited means were still able to own the simple mills or, in other words, the tools of industry. But now, with the arrival of the steam engine, the shop became a factory, too expensive to be owned by a simple master workman of the older regime. So, just at this point, the modern capitalist appeared.

There is, of course, no inherent necessity for the machines to be owned by private capitalists. They might be, and in many instances are, owned by the public, as in municipal plants of various kinds. It happened, however, that England, who took the lead in the new industrial system, was not then so socially minded as she and many other nations are today. So those individuals who were able and ready to do so were permitted to capture the new inventions for their own enrichment. They were, to be sure, already rich in a sense, or they could not have built and owned new factories. Those who were in position to do this had made their money through trade and banking in the period just preceding, and a few of them were the hereditary proprietors of great landed estates, which included not only open country but even villages in some cases. Having *had* more they were in position to *get* more. They became the builders and owners of the new factories, which included the tools within them. The workmen no longer had the least voice in directing their own work, working hours, or working conditions. They were called to work by the factory whistle, and when it failed to blow they had no work and no wages. As they truly complained at the time, although unheeded, the new machine system had "separated the worker from his tools." With a deep understanding of the drift of things, they rose up against the new machines and smashed them to pieces in many disorderly scenes. Their more highly educated employers, and the learned economists who upheld and explained the new industrial order, laughed them to scorn and proved to their own satisfaction that those ignorant workmen were blind and foolish. Yet subsequent history has shown that they were wiser in some ways, though not in all, than their masters. For a time the critics seemed right, for the workman had a job despite the fact that he no longer owned or controlled the tools with which he had to work. But now, after a century and a half, he has neither tools nor job in the case of tens of millions of men and women, even in the most wealthy nations.

Moreover, there are profound students of the situation who say that, even when the best times of which our industrial system is capable return, there will be from ten to twenty millions unemployed all the time. How can such things be? Incredible as it seems, this is the outlook as seen by practically all those most qualified to speak; and that means those who have devoted themselves to the study of the social sciences and who have no selfish interest in keeping things as they now are. Yet, in order to understand their predictions, it is necessary for us to notice one or two more links in the story of man and his tools, particularly his machines.

Automatic machinery. As long as machines were used to lighten toil for men and required workmen to run them, there was little ground for complaint. But very early in its career the new power-driven machinery began to take the place of human workers to a greater and greater degree. This needs no argument, because it is common knowledge, known for about a hundred years. On every side one hears, and has long heard, employers expressing their pride in new machines that are "almost human," and can "do the work of ten (or twenty or some greater number) of men." We do not assume, of course, that such machines displaced all the men from a given shop or from industry in general. It is true that many of the displaced workers are re-employed in the making of other machines. These are used in making the machines that took their former jobs. So on down the line to the enlarged mines and other basic industries required to supply the raw materials used in the building of machines, which make other machines; and so on back up the line. The important fact is, however, often overlooked—that, since each new machine in the line uses relatively fewer workers, there is bound to be an unwanted surplus of them when the end of the line is reached. And that is where the army of unemployed in another line, namely, the bread line, is recruited.

Automatic self-tending machinery. At every step in the long process from the first hammerstone and chipped flint to the most elaborate modern machines, man was separated, as we have shown, ever farther and farther from his tools, and eventually from his job. The final step has come very recently. It was in the fall of 1932, when the group of engineers and economists known as *Technocrats* made known their astounding studies, covering more than ten years, that the public began to realize that automatic machinery had created a new and critical situation in the Western world. Along with a wealth of statistical evidence showing how modern machines have steadily increased their total product at the very same time that they were using less human labor, it was revealed that the automatic processes had done even more incredible things. There are now, it was shown, machines that oil themselves; turn their driving power on or off by electrical devices; feed themselves with raw materials; sort, inspect, wrap, and carry away their own product, casting aside all imperfect units; and do even more wonderful things as in the case of the Robot, or Mechanical Man. As a result of all this, there was pictured a projected rayon factory without a single workman in it. Labor had been completely separated from the machine and from the job, as far as that shop was concerned; and a number of other shops equally empty of men are said to exist.

In these complex, power-driven, automatic, self-tending, "almost human" machines, we see the final work of a race of beings who have intelligence enough to invent their way from clubs and chipped flints to automatic factories, but not enough intelligence, so far as yet shown, to create social inventions that will make the machine the servant of all the members of the society which alone made it possible. When it is seen thus in the long perspective of history, it is clear that technological employment is one of the most acute problems of the present hour—but it is the outcome of a process that began thousands of years ago, when the cave man chipped his first flint.*

*Reprinted from *Sociology and Social Research*, 20:8-17, September-October, 1935.

TOOLS AND CULTURE*

IF WE APPROACH the problem of civilization without the academic dread of offending Darwinian unilinear evolution, the unity of nature, or other vested interests of the academic world, our method will be more truly objective, and the task before us may find itself considerably simplified. Even at that, it must prove difficult enough, for the reason that culture, or civilization if preferred, is a highly complex thing even in its most primitive and simplest forms. Nevertheless, it is the datum with which all the social sciences and other humanistic disciplines have to begin. The fact that many writers in these fields have approached their own subjects through long and imposing corridors of biological and psychological reasoning, leading through the domain of purely animal behavior, does not change the location of the front doorsill, so far as the social sciences are concerned. History, political science, economics, anthropology, sociology, philosophy, and all their company carry by assumption the word *human* before them so unequivocally that it is superfluous to utter it. Very recently those interested in reducing all things to common categories have sought to extend the sociological interpretation and inquiry to the subhuman world. Already two significant results have appeared, one being the fact that a new term, "animal sociology," has been found necessary; the other, that the two sociologies have little, if anything, in common. Thus, in a very recent chapter on "Mammalian Sociology," an eminent anatomist says, after extended firsthand observations of monkeys and apes:

Culture . . . is an essentially human phenomenon. It is conceivable that a clearer biological understanding of the nature of speech and its derivatives will eventually bring the materials of sociology within the scope of physiological interpretation. Meanwhile, however, a significant and convenient line of demarcation can be drawn between the respective fields of human and animal sociology.[1]

Others have extended their investigations to the study of the social insects, notably termites, ants, wasps, and bees,

---

*Reprinted by permission from *The Personalist*, 13:245-60, October, 1932.

[1] S. Zuckerman, *The Social Life of Monkeys and Apes* (New York, 1932), Chap. II, especially p. 19. Dr. Zuckerman is Anatomist to the Zoological Society of London and Demonstrator of Anatomy, University College, London.

and here we meet the phrase "insect sociology." But in this field, even more than in that of the anthropoid primates, the difference in mode of life from that of human groups is so great that the word sociology itself is almost all the two sciences have in common. There is, of course, the formal fact that creatures of all orders live together. They have associates, companions, *socii*, and in that sense they possess society. Since "sociology" in its generic sense means the study or science of the social group, it is not improper to extend it to the examination of subhuman primates, and even of lower animal forms on the level of the insects or still simpler organisms. But the most significant thing thus far emerging from all such inquiries is their uniform tendency to throw human cultural society into clear relief as a distinct and unique order of phenomena.

The elaborate social organism of the beehive has been described by many able writers, by none more instructively and eloquently than Maurice Maeterlinck in his really classical book, *The Life of the Bee*. He finds therein "a perfectly diabolical intelligence," so efficient yet so different from our own that it arouses feelings akin to fear when contemplated. The specialization of functions among those "monarchical socialists," as he aptly dubs them, is amazing, with its architects and builders of cells, its pollen gatherers, nectar bringers, doorkeepers, ventilators, drones, queen and her bodyguard, nymphs, and all the rest.

Alongside the beehive let us place the anthill, with its captive aphids and captor ants of various orders, its concerted, rhythmic, almost choral labor, its engineering, slave-holding, stock-raising, warring activities — the whole a marvel of social solidarity and cooperation fascinating to naturalists and sociologists alike. Yet all this is rooted in morphological and instinctive adaptation to the environment in both its physical and social aspects. Those creatures are literally *built for* their specific social order and their own individual roles within it. In his monumental work on *The Social World of the Ants*, Henri Forel remarks that there are seventy-five hundred different species, races, and varieties of ants, each with its specific instincts. This condition, when augmented by the numerous morphological variations within each species, raises the number to twenty-four thousand or more different kinds of ants.[2]

Here we behold social adjustment and vocational adaptation carried to the highest degree. For instance, such investigators as Forel mention, in a single hill, a class of big, strong-limbed ants specially built to drag leaves to the colony, where a second group with exceptionally huge and powerful jaws chop the leaves into large segments. These pieces in turn are minced to a fine mulch by still others characterized by small and rapidly operating jaws. All these structurally different ant classes are cooperating toward the single end of providing a suitable culture medium for the growing of a certain kind of fungus designed as infant food for the oncoming generation. The ant may be said to have "a head for his job" in the above instance, and even more literally so in the case of the "doorkeeper ant," whose special vocation is to block the entrance to the den, situated in a rotten tree limb, by thrusting his huge overgrown head, shaped exactly to fit, into the entrance tunnel, bored by the queen mother when she first entered and prepared to lay the eggs that represented the future colony! This colony, when it hatches out, develops among others of different type sons whose oversized heads exactly fit the opening, in respect to size, shape, color, and texture;[3] and these constitute the doorkeeper class.

Not only is the basis of such societies known to be instinctive and structural at bottom, but naturalists have pointed out that the presence of neuters, that is, sexually undeveloped individuals, presents the key to insect society. An insufficient nourishment supplied by their parents to these individuals causes in them a morphological modification, namely, an atrophied condition of the sex organs. This results in a partial suppression of their instincts. The desire to mate is sublimated in an altruistic devotion to the offspring of their sexually developed siblings. Consequently, they partially starve themselves, and so remain sexless, while they lavish upon the young of others the gatherings of their labor.

In social aggregates of this kind we behold a type of behavior essentially different from that of human groups. The

---

[2] Henri Forel, *The Social World of the Ants* (C. K. Ogden's translation; New York, 1928), Vol. I, p. 42.

[3] *Ibid.*, Vol. II. p. 289.

eggs of any insect swarm, carried halfway around the globe, will hatch into creatures who repeat in all its elaborate details the social arrangements of ancestors whom they never saw. Indeed, that is what happens in the regular course of events among the wood-boring beetles and the seventeen-year locusts. The wood borer lives its own life, lays its eggs and dies, passing from the scene before its young are born. These in due time hatch out, enter untaught upon the same round of social activities, and follow exactly in the footsteps of ancestors of whose existence they can have no knowledge by any process known to us. Without father or mother, without sons or daughters, they live in an eternal present, perfectly adjusted to their own familiar social world of contemporaries, and also to two social worlds of which they are apparently completely unaware, namely, their own ancestors and descendants.

If we couple with this fact, as noted above, the related fact that bodily structure determines behavior among such creatures, we may conclude that their behavior has repeated itself without modification for millions of years, as revealed by the bodies of ants once entangled and buried in the resin of primeval pine trees and preserved for our eyes in that same gum petrified by milleniums into our present-day amber. Their living descendants probably act just as their fathers did a million generations ago, and doubtless the wood-boring beetles are doing likewise, but in one sense there has been but a single generation during all that vast lapse of intervening time.

In behavior of this type, which is never learned and never forgotten, which moves by untaught methods to an unforeseen end, there is exemplified the internal storage of race experience, registered in the germ plasm, and operating by means of instinctive behavior patterns. It bridges a time gap during which no fully developed and really living member of the race exists, being carried across solely by the tendencies inhering in the germ plasm and only partially expressed in the inert and slumbering larval beings.

In the case of the higher animals one faces a different situation. They also live in groups and manifest social behavior of the instinctive order in the main, but with important modifications. Here the lives of the generations overlap the example of older individuals, and even their instruction and training, becomes a factor, and the experience of the individual is supplemented by that of a continuous and never-dying group. In this respect a flock of birds or a herd of cattle presents a social phenomenon of an order quite distinct from that of a swarm of insects. Consequently a new level of life emerges, namely, that marked by the internal storage of individual and parental experience, registered in the somatoplasm, particularly the individual nervous system, and operating by means of habit patterns. . . . .

In the two ways indicated experience is stored by animals, thereby enabling them to carry the past forward with them into the future. Time really counts with them, for like all living organisms they are "time-binders," to borrow Count Korzybski's phrase. They are different now by virtue of what they were then, having stored within themselves tendencies to act which cause them to contribute to any behavior situation an element which transcends a purely mechanical description or explanation. If one propels a toy frog with the toe of his boot across the floor, its speed and direction are predictable in terms of the force and angle of each thrust and the resistance of the floor. Replace the porcelain frog with a live one and all calculations become mere guesses, inasmuch as a frog of this sort may leap into the air or straight at the aggressor, according to tendencies stored up within his skin. These may be the instinctive behavior patterns of his race or species, or the habit patterns formed through his own experience and that of his immediate associates. Both of these are internal storages, the one in the germ plasm, the other in the nervous system.

Man possesses both the patterns already described, and a third one besides, the last being peculiar to his kind. This is the external storage of communal experience, registered in the form of tools and symbols, and operating by means of social values with their corresponding attitudes in persons. This third form of experience storage[4] deals with social

---

[4] I am indebted to Professor L. L. Bernard for this idea of the storage of experience. It has been stimulating to my thought, but he is not to be held responsible for the particular use of it made here. See his paper entitled "Factors Basic to the Evolution of Culture," in the *American Journal of Sociology*, 32:177-205, September, 1926; also "The Classification of Culture," in *Sociology and Social Research*, 15:209-29, January-February, 1931.

values and is the distinguishing process of human, as contrasted with subhuman, forms of life. Insects of the type
described inherit nothing from former generations except
their bodily form and the instinctive behavior patterns that
go with such bodies. All this is transmitted across the time
gap from generation to generation. The higher animals
receive this heritage and also whatever is learned by direct
personal contact with the parent generation. This second
form of heritage cannot bridge a time gap, however brief,
so that experience won by any individual dies with him unless
transmitted by direct contact to his imitators.

Not so with the third method. It is entirely outside the
germ plasm and also outside the individual, in so far as it
exists in the form of tools and symbols. It is in that sense
superindividual, and also in the sense that it is created in
groups and is transmitted only through groups. It is, as
already said, *communal* experience, using the word communal
to denote not only one's contemporaries but also his ancestors
and forerunners in general. The possessor of culture lives his
life in common with men and women who vanished from the
earthly scene hundreds or thousands of years ago. The stored
experience of countless generations becomes in part the experience of all who understand the meaningful group objects,
material and spiritual, which constitute the social values of
the community in question, and who share the attitudes which
the group takes toward them. This is what Pascal had in
mind, no doubt, in his famous saying that "the whole series of
human generations during the course of the ages should be
regarded as one man ever living and ever learning."[5]

It is literally true that any one of us may be closer in spirit
to men or women of a thousand years ago than to people he
meets every day. This is possible without the mediation of
those contemporaries themselves. So Petrarch, advance agent
of the Renaissance in Italy, used to lie upon some lofty Roman
ruin under the blue Italian sky and wonder what race of intellectual giants reared those imposing structures, while down
below him, as he mused, neighboring peasants were busily

---

[5]Quoted by Professor McQuilken De Grange in the critical "Appen-
dix" to his translation of Turgot's essay, *On the Progress of the Human
Mind* (Hanover, N. H.: The Sociological Press, 1929). De Grange
quotes thus from Pascal, who anticipated Turgot in the idea, usually
attributed to the latter.

quarrying the hewn blocks from the walls and carting them away for the building of hen coops and pigsties. When Petrarch, by the aid of Chrysoloras, brought over from Greece, learned to read the Greek language, he and his contemporaries were enabled to pass through the pages of long-neglected and musty parchments into the long-vanished life of the Golden Age that produced Socrates, Plato, and Aristotle, and to commune with them across the chasm of a thousand years and more.

Nowhere have I seen so striking an example of this power of culture experience to transcend the ages than in the following incidents related to Professor René Worms by Achilles Ouiy, his editorial associate on the staff of the *Revue Internationale de Sociologie:*

When he made to me his final recommendations concerning the Sociological Society, the Wednesday which preceded his end, he expressed his desire to live a few hours longer in order to know what was said at the session of the society, which met that same evening! Then divining no doubt the emotion that agitated me, he wished not himself to yield in the least, and, smiling, he related to me, in the Greek text, a short passage from the *Phaedo*, on "the fine hazard of the great departure." Then, without weakening, he made with the hand a gesture of friendly dismissal, a cordial signal of definite farewell.[*]

In this instance we see Worms, a French scholar of our own times, sustaining himself in the hour of death with the recollection of the sublimely heroic experience and teaching of Socrates twenty-five hundred years before, and quoting his immortal words in the very language in which they were first spoken. In the face of such incomparable experiences it seems absurd to discuss seriously the contention of those who seek to claim for animals also any comparable part in culture heritage. Not that one would arbitrarily exclude them, or deny their strikingly intelligent doings, which we shall have occasion to recount in a later passage; but simply because their mode of life is evidently of a different order. The very large majority of thinkers in every field of science would seem to recognize in culture a distinctive, even if not absolutely exclusive, human trait. The fact is well attested. Our next task is to explain, if possible, just how this holds true.

In discussions of this problem, the definition with which one

---

[*]In the *Revue Internationale de Sociologie*, 33:580, 1925.

sets out is highly important for the conclusion. In Hart and Pantzer's admirable paper they define culture as "behavior patterns socially acquired and socially transmitted," and proceed to show that subhuman animals possess such patterns and manifest such behavior. If we may accept the facts as established, which is not perfectly certain, it follows that animals possess culture in the sense defined. But in that event behavior of a distinctly different order among humans remains over and unexplained. We are consequently left to choose between calling the animal behavior described by them "cultural" and seeking a new term for denoting human behavior; or, on the other hand, deciding to call the animal behavior in question "subcultural" and to reserve the word culture, as most thinkers do, for behavior of the distinctive human type. In this discussion I choose the latter course because thus only can one do justice to both the ascertained facts and the established terminology.

In order to escape a battle of mere words we need to stick closely to our analysis of the three types of experience storage, whereupon it becomes quite plain that animals below man have not been found, in a natural condition, to be possessors of our third form of heritage. Culture is whatsoever man (or any other creature) has learned as a member of society, has stored externally and transmitted socially, by means of tools and symbols, in the form of social values together with their corresponding attitudes in persons. This is the storage of communal experience in the third form set forth in an earlier passage. Its essence consists in tools and symbols, and to an attempt at the analysis of such things this discussion must next be directed. And here again an examination of subhuman behavior will probably shed most light, not for its own sake, but as setting forth by contrast the significance of the tool in human behavior.

Bergson's early remarks on this question, which is producing a considerable discussion of late, have not been surpassed. Referring to the well-known collections of anecdotes on the intelligence of animals he concludes that those nearest man, such as apes and elephants, "can use an artificial instrument occasionally." Those lower down can *recognize* a constructed object, for instance a trap. None of them invent or construct artificial instruments, although "towards that achievement the intelligence of animals tends as toward an ideal." He seems to think that man is really more of a maker than a thinker, the original feature of human intelligence being "the faculty of manufacturing artificial objects, especially tools to make tools, and of indefinitely varying the manufacture." Then he propounds and answers the crucial question:

Does an intelligent animal also possess tools or machines? Yes, certainly, but here the instrument forms a part of the body that uses it; and, corresponding to this instrument, there is an *instinct* that knows how to use it.[7]

The notable work by Köhler on *The Mentality of Apes* contains many profound observations made at the ape colony in Teneriffe, Northwest Africa. Hornaday, in his interesting volume, *The Mind and Manners of Wild Animals*, based largely upon personal observations, gives many fascinating accounts that clearly reveal a surprising intelligence in various species, although one finds few if any evidences of tool-using capacity and none of their fabrication. In the delightful, photographically illustrated studies by Enos A. Mills in his book entitled *In Beaver World*, the elaborate and extensive operations of the colony are so clearly shown to be the adaptation of means to ends that it can hardly be explained by instinct. The Indian tailor bird is also one of the most promising claimants to tool-using intelligence, as described by observers in Ceylon.[8] Her work is said to include the four distinct processes of sewing, riveting, lacing, and matting.

If we lay aside the examples of animals under the direct care of man and consider only those in a wild state, where the case must rest, it appears that their work consists in the modification of environment by the direct action of their own organs, without the mediation of any instrumentality whatsoever. Even the often-mentioned trap-door spider follows the direct method, and her gossamer-lined tunnel, trap door included, is after all simply a highly ingenious and elaborately finished nest. The same has to be said of the beavers. Their marvelous colonies, dams, ponds, canals, and houses should be regarded as a huge nest, in the sense that it consists of nothing

---

[7]Henri Bergson, *Creative Evolution* (Mitchell's translation; New York, 1911 and 1924), pp. 138, 139.
[8]*Cf.* Casey A. Wood, "The Nest of the Indian Tailor Bird," *Annual Report* of the Smithsonian Institution, 1925, pp. 349-54.

else than the natural environment as modified and shaped by
the unaided organs of the beavers themselves. The only ex-
ceptions that have come to my notice are the use of a pebble
by the hammer beetle to tamp down the loose earth around
her doorway and the utilization of her own larvae by the ant,
Camponotus senex, as a sort of shuttle for the weaving of her
web, that insect being able to spin threads only in the larval
stage.

In these two cases only does the animal make use of anything that could be regarded as partaking of the nature of a
tool. For a tool is essentially an abstraction and an instrumentality, and not an organ. Animal tools in Bergson's sense
are simply organs. They are natural, not artificial. The organ
is grown by nature, but the tool is devised by the wit of its
user. The simplest form of devising is simply the selecting
of the suitable object when it lies at hand, be it a spinning
larva, or a pebble, or some other thing suited to work in hand.
Animal achievement does not reach even this lowest stage
except in the possible instance of the hammer beetle's pebble
and the larva shuttle of *Camponotus senex,* and other ant
species.[*]

Whatever may be thought of the typical or atypical character of these instances, at the next stage, namely, that where
tools are deliberately fabricated, the entire world of subhuman
creatures is left behind. This fact is itself less important
than the conditions that account for it, for in them we shall
find the secret of the tool and of culture.

All the evidence points to the conclusion that the experience
of creatures below man is an undifferentiated concrete whole,
into which the animal is merged as an integral part incapable
of separating itself in consciousness, and hence having no
room for any mediator or instrumentality between its own
organs and the aspects of nature with which they correlate.
Bergson developed this thought with incomparable insight
and lucidity in his *Creative Evolution.*

The animal and its environment are one. It floats in the
stream of pure duration as a fish floats in the river unaware
of the river or of itself as such. Man prates about being "a
part of all that I have met"; the instinctive animal does not

---

[*]Forel, *op. cit.,* pp. 280-82.

poetize about it but just *is* that. You and I lived that way for some years, and probably our earliest memories have to do with stressful experiences where the bright mirror of life's smoothly flowing stream was momentarily shattered as the conscious ego began to emerge. . . . .

Animal instinct operates by *synthesis* and apprehends the *concrete;* human intelligence pursues *analysis* and ends with the *abstract*. The one walks with life; the other traces the footprints left by life. The method of human intelligence is to *abstract* from the total situation one or more single aspects of it. The primary and ever-present form that this takes with us is to set *ourselves* over against the physical or social environment, as something distinct from it or opposed to it in varying degrees of sharpness. One cannot imagine a beaver as operating upon its environment. It *is* the environment, at least to the degree that the beaver works within it rather than upon it. It uses the organs that have *grown* by the interaction of the life forces in the configuration or *gestalt* which includes equally the beaver and the thing that we spatially thinking humans speak of as its environment. In consequence of this we take to tools, which are, it is true, extensions of our natural organs (the primitive hammerstone a magnified fist, the club an extended arm, the war club a magnified fist on an extended arm), but they are more than extensions. A tool is essentially an abstraction and the servant of abstraction. Whereas the beaver expeditiously gnaws down trees with its own sharp teeth, primitive man gnaws them down laboriously with his dull flint axe and thereby introduces a free-floating factor which is not confined to trees or to its owner. It is tied up to no specific situation, but works anywhere within a vast number of situations of the generic chopping type. Thus every tool is, in the most literal sense, an abstraction.

It is not so obvious that a tool is also a symbol,[10] but reflection will show that it is. This may be facilitated by observing first that a symbol is itself a tool—a tool of the mind. Language, mathematics, and logical methods were explicitly so

---

[10] Professor L. L. Bernard says, "All physical inventions are in a sense forms of writing, because they become symbolic controls for the mediation of adjustment responses." *American Journal of Sociology,* 32:198, September, 1926.

called by Lester F. Ward in his *Pure Sociology,* and it is clear
why that is true. Just as an axe is an instrumentality interposed between the human body and some portion of the physical environment, likewise a symbol is an instrumentality interposed between the mind and its social environment. In the
one case, the activity of the user modifies, through the tool,
his physical surroundings. In the other, his activity affects,
through the symbol, his social and mental environment. A
symbol is therefore a tool whereby the agent, abstracted by
virtue of his waking-being from the total life situation, operates to bring himself back into closer communion with it.
Moreover, it is in the nature of a symbol to stand for something besides itself and to be freely interchangeable in countless situations, as in the infinitude of words that can be spelled
with the twenty-six letters of a single alphabet, or the countless truths and falsities that can be demonstrated by means of
the same formal reasoning. All this is plainly true of symbols,
but it is true, though not quite so obviously, also of tools.
They, for example an axe, stand for something besides themselves. Who wants an axe that no longer cuts things? It is
no longer an axe. But as long as it is an axe it stands for
chopped trees and other desired goods. Finally, like any
letter of the alphabet it will work freely in every situation—
no matter how long and varied the list—where its nature
enables it to serve life activities, more explicitly human
activities. So in the twofold sense that it is mediatory and
interchangeable a tool is a symbol. Conversely a symbol is a
tool; and both are the product and the producers of abstraction, the hallmark of intelligence and waking-being. This is
both good and bad. It gives to man the glory of being the
only *maker* in the created world—Bergson would substitute
as our zoological designation *Homo faber* for *Homo sapiens.*
He thus implies that we are makers rather than thinkers, but
man is the latter also—perhaps too much so—and Shakespeare
might just as truly have said, considering the spiritual famine
that threatens our race, "Yon *Homo* hath a lean and hungry
look. He thinks too much."

MACHINES AND CIVILIZATION*

A TOOL is any device of simple, unitary character that is dependent for its motion upon the bodily movements of a living organism. This is always a human being, except for the rare instances ascribed to animals, particularly those in a tamed or domesticated condition. As the preceding essay tried to show, the tool even in this simplest form is an abstraction, a "drawing away" from some concrete whole or life configuration of the tool wielder and the tool. The instinctive animal is merged in consciousness and activity with its environment, while man sets himself self-consciously over against the environment and operates upon it not directly but indirectly, not immediately but by means of a mediator. The mediator in such behavior is what we call in English a *tool*, the word running back, according to the lexicographers, through Icelandic to Gothic roots which meant "to do" or "to make," or even "to tan" (leather). This has its significance for our discussion because it shows how intimately the tool in its primitive form was part of the user. In a real sense it was an extension not only of his body but also of his personality. In this connection it is interesting to note Dr. Otis T. Mason's remark that the ivory handles of Eskimo scrapers and other implements "fit so exactly that the white man, with his much larger hands, is unable to use them."[1] Such tools, being limited in their interchangeability, are thereby integral parts of a concrete situation and consequently saved to that extent from degenerating into complete abstractions. Professor De Laguna has expressed this personal intimacy of the genuine tool in the following vivid words:

The tool has been called an extension of the human organism, bound up with the skeletal frame and with the muscular and nervous systems, as if it had been produced by the same processes of reproduction and growth. As the blind man feels with his cane just as if the nerve-endings of his fingertips were really at the end of the wooden stick; so the skillful joiner handles the mallet and chisel, modulating the force of the blow and adjusting the cutting-angle with the same ease

*Reprinted by permission from *The Personalist*, 14:11-30, January, 1933.

[1]*Cf*. Otis T. Mason, *The Origins of Invention* (New York, 1910), p. 35.

and certainty and spontaneity with which he chews and swallows his food.[2]

In this fine passage one is led to sense the joy of fine craftsmanship such as once reigned among the gilds of Europe, and which still lives in simpler economic orders. An example is that of the Indian pottery maker of a Mexican village who, as described by Professor William Kirk, will reject a high price on the road in order to complete his pilgrimage to the distant market and offer his wares for sale at a lower price before

an admiring group of fellow craftsmen and townspeople who have recognized his skill in the past . . . All the time he is fashioning his earthen pots and jars, he carries in his mind a picture of the future scene in which he expects to be the principal actor . . . living, as he does, in a simple economic order, he is able to feel the thrill of creative workmanship.[3]

But the tool does not linger always in its pristine state of intimate union with the body and mind of its wielder. Its first departure is, however, a short and simple one; and with it we find simple, and still intimate, tools in which one part moves another, as in a pair of pincers, or a pulley with its rope. But in this case the human wielder is the prime mover and dominates the process.

At the next stage he is shoved into the background, and the forces of nature become the motive power in his stead. The *machine* emerges, as the power-driven tool, and starts on its triumphant career as the disintegrating factor in modern life according to some, as the instrument of all progress according to others. There is probably a core of truth in both contentions, but we cannot pursue that discussion here except in so far as it bears upon the significance of analysis *versus* synthesis, of the abstract as against the concrete, in our modern social life. It should be remarked, however, in passing, that the most thoughtful students of the problem show a helpful tendency to make discrimination among the many kinds of machines with which we have to do.

After all is said and done, the basic truth I am emphasizing cannot be denied, although its moral and social effects may be

[2]Theodore de Laguna, *The Factors of Social Evolution* (New York, 1926), p. 192.

[3]*Cf.* William Kirk, "Cultural Conflict in Mexican Life," *Sociology and Social Research,* 15:352-64, March-April, 1931.

variously evaluated. The machine is a long stride, indeed a
whole series of them, in this abstracting process. At first,
nothing stood between the doer and his deed. Then the tool
was interposed between the natural organ and that aspect of
surroundings on which it worked. Next a series of moving
parts was interpolated, and as it grew in length the creative
workman was shoved, as prime mover, farther and farther
away from his product. Finally an engine of some sort, by
which is meant a device utilizing the forces of nature, such as
wind, waterfall, or steam, is substituted for the original doer;
and now we use the phrase "prime mover" to mean not a man
but an *engine*. Shortly after that orgy of mechanization in
industry which we know in English history as the Industrial
Revolution, the socialists raised their cry that the machine
had "separated the workman from his tools." They referred
primarily to the fact that the workman's kit of privately
owned hand tools had been replaced by the huge steam-driven
and water-driven machines owned by the capitalist, and usable
only at his beck and call. This is, of course, true and deplorable, but an even greater evil, not then perceived by socialists
other than the social and philosophic seers like Kingsley,
Carlyle, Ruskin, and Morris, was lurking in the new appa-
ratus. That was its capacity for disintegrating the socio-
economic configuration expressed in the manorial and guild
life, and for canceling more and more completely the human
element from industrial production, no matter who succeeded
in owning the machines.

Thenceforth social atomism became increasingly the order
of the day, first in economic relations, then in all the affairs
of life. As Garet Garrett has demonstrated with masterful
logic in his *Ouroboros, or the Mechanical Extension of Mankind*,[4] power-driven machinery does not cheapen production,
but actually increases the cost of the product except where a
large quantity of output decreases the cost per unit. This
explains why a modern machine-equipped industry unceas-
ingly strives for a larger output, on the principle that the
larger the volume the cheaper the units and the bigger the
sales. But a large output by machine methods requires that
the product be standardized, or made exactly alike, in size,

---

[4] In the "Today and Tomorrow Series" (New York, n.d.).

shape, texture, and color, with, of course, some variation between large sections of the total run; the more variation the worse, from the point of view of machine industry. These units and parts of units, being thus standardized, are interchangeable. So also are the machines themselves, their several parts, and the human part likewise, in some places completely, in others largely, and in others only slightly, but in every case to a certain extent, and over and above the slight interchangeability that inheres in human beings themselves for the less personal and less unique relations of life. There is enough of John Doe in all of us at best, and the machine has made matters worse by magnifying it.

Large-scale machine production has divorced the industrial process from *creative production,* as already shown. It has also tended to destroy something equally valuable, namely, *selective consumption.* Where the machine triumphs, the workman is not the only one whose initiative is impaired or destroyed. The same is true of the *consumer* of the output in constantly increasing degree. He cannot choose to wear clothing that is not to be found in any store, or follow styles that the mode makers do not render available. Moreover, his very standards of taste, not only in dress and furnishings but in eating and drinking, are manufactured for him by joint control of producing and advertising on the part of the machine masters. Just who the masters are in this case does not appear, since the movement toward specialization, division of labor, atomization, and anonymity has involved the managers. One finds more and more of the separate parts, and less and less of the configuration. The *gestalt,* the total situation, becomes more elusive. So the machine, like the centurion in the Scripture, might well say, "I also am a man set under authority, having under myself soldiers: and I say to this one, Go, and he goeth; and to another, Come, and he cometh; and to my servant, Do this, and he doeth it."[5]

The machine we have seen hailed, and rightly, as "the symbol of the new age," but, as the German philosopher-sociologist Georg Simmel profoundly observes, "it is in *money* that the modern spirit finds its most perfect expression." We are indebted to Dr. Nicholas Spykman for his notable translation

---

[5]Luke 7:8.

and systematization of Simmel's numerous and widely scat-
tered contributions, in the volume entitled *The Social Theory
of Georg Simmel.*[6]

The philosophy of Simmel differs from that of the writer
in so far as he sees in money the supreme means to the differentiation and liberation of the individual. Even there the
point of view here expounded takes no exception so long as
liberation is meant to denote that social process which accomplishes merely the atomization of society in an external way,
without implying any increase of real personal freedom, as
Simmel seems to hold in numerous passages. Professor Edward A. Ross calls it "Individuation,"[7] in his chapter by that
title, and defines it by saying: "The processes which pulverize
social lumps and release the action of their members may be
termed *individuation.*"[8]   He then proceeds to sketch the
breakup of the ancient Teutonic *kindred,* the Chinese *clan,*
and the Roman *family* of the *patria potestas* type. It would
seem that Simmel most penetratingly elaborates the money
economy in its sociological and philosophical aspects. For
instance, the German thinker, being both philosopher and
sociologist, and consequently a true *social philosopher* when
he cared to assume that role, treats of money and intellect in
identical terms. Speaking of "the significance of money and
intelligence for modern life," he is translated by Spykman
as follows:

Both lack character. Both are merely functions. Intelligence is
the indifferent mirror of the actuality in which all elements are pictured with complete indifference as to their values. In their relation
to intelligence all elements have equal rights as long as they are actual.
Money is an indifferent mirror in which all elements are pictured with
complete indifference to all nonmonetary values. In their relation to
money, all elements have equal rights as long as they have an economic
value.

This lack of character which is the essence of both money and
intellect, is also manifest in a more positive aspect. Money shows its
complete indifference to other values in being available for all purposes.
It serves the noblest pursuits and the basest desires, it functions in
enterprises for human welfare as well as in enterprises for human

---

[6]Nicholas Spykman, *The Social Theory of Georg Simmel* (Chicago,
1925), p. 251.

[7]Edward A. Ross, *Principles of Sociology* (New York, 1920).

[8]*Ibid.,* p. 439.

destruction. In a similar fashion intelligence is used both for the welfare of humanity and for theft and murder.[9]

The objectivity which he thus depicts in both intellect and money Simmel finds to be no new quality which they have merely added on to other qualities. He distinctly declares that "it is their very essence." Moreover, he points out in so many words that "this objective and impersonal character of money and intellect is also responsible for their importance in the development of individualism."

These truths are apparent to all who have reflected on modern life; so it is not necessary to support our own observations with a further array of authority. It is of value, however, in this way to suggest that we are not exploiting a merely private opinion or whimsy. Everything in Simmel's remarkable discussion is true at bottom simply because of the fact that money is not anything in itself, being merely a universally recognized and hence freely exchangeable *symbol* for economic goods and services in general. We should note also that it seems to indicate as a corollary that a *coin* is not money in the purest and strictest sense because the metal in it has a definite economic value based on its utility and scarcity when regarded simply as a piece of useful metal of the given weight. The true money is really the paper tokens and instruments of credit, which, aside from their symbolic value, are not actually worth the paper they are printed on, having no utility in themselves. Money thus becomes the culmination of that abstracting process which we have traced, beginning with the first tool of the hand, passing to tools of the mind or symbols, advancing to machines, first hand driven and then power driven, passing on into specialization, division of labor, the divorcement of the worker from his tools, of the maker from his creative relation to the product, of the consumer from his selective function respecting the product, and culminating in the economy of money as the supreme abstraction and pure symbol of economic functions as such, in entire disconnection from personal relations or social values. The money system thus becomes the algebra of the modern industrial regime, being characterized by symbols for quantities, known or unknown,

[9]Spykman, *op. cit.*, p. 234.

toward whose individual content, or absolute value, the symbols are indifferent. The money economy represents the equations of impersonal claims to economic functions.

All this completely sustains, in general, our thesis with respect to the drift from primitive concreteness and synthesis to the modern abstractions created by analysis, which is pre-eminently the method of intellect and science. Moreover, the particular tendency of modern industrial civilization to reduce even the workman to standardized and interchangeable parts is aptly illustrated in a further remark by Simmel. Thus he shows how the individual, supplied with money, gains "an inner independency, a feeling of individual self-sufficiency. His freedom," he explicitly declares, "consists in his *ability to change the individuals on whom he shall depend.*"[10] Let us next see how this tallies with our own knowledge of "savage" and civilized life.

In describing the social organization of the Trobriand Islanders, a recent anthropological writer gives a picture of social control as it operates in the life of one of the forest clans, even to formal "sending away" (banishment) of the chief's own son, through popular consensus.[11]

In *Natural Man*, by Charles H. Hose,[12] one reads a similar description of the tribes of Borneo. Those preliterate people occupy together a communal building similar to the long house of our own Iroquois Indians, although vastly more populous. It is set high upon foundation posts on the river banks, and faces the river, with its long side parallel to the stream. This side is open, and amounts to a very long partially enclosed porch where occur the mending of nets, fashioning of weapons, and the hundred and one activities of work and play that go on in any group of several hundred intimately associated human beings. Yet in those crowded quarters excellent order prevails, under social control as centered in the tribal headman or chief. Since clashes are not infrequent and disorder is a constant possibility, it is interesting to note just how that communal head exerts his authority and preserves order. His leadership rests on

---

Ibid., p. 221 (italics mine).

"Cf. Bronislaw Malinowski, *Crime and Custom in Savage Society* (New York, 1926), pp. 100-4.

"Charles H. Hose, *Natural Man* (London and New York, 1926).

ability, fairness, and public confidence. The procedure is simple. If any member should prove insubordinate, which, I believe, does not occur, he might be commanded, I fancy, simply *to get off the platform* as a sufficient punishment— to us, at first glance, a trivial thing, but really equivalent to getting off the life raft at sea. The house was not set upon posts to no purpose, for down there on the dank ground the jungle swarms with venomous insects and deadly serpents, not to mention other ferocious beasts that day and night seek their prey. If our fancied outcast were to escape, by any chance, those perils, and come safely through the jungle, he might encounter the weapons of a hostile tribe, and perish at their hands.

In a word, there is no place for him to live except upon the communal platform, and there he usually remains, paying the price of that submission prescribed by public sentiment and enforced under the ecological sanctions of the jungle situation. This case is merely typical of primitive society everywhere.

Now let us contrast with this the outlook for a recalcitrant youth in our modern civilized society. He has only to possess a store of cash, which he may have received by way of gift, have stolen, or, quite improbable at his years, have earned and saved. With that he can disobey his parents, defy his teachers, hoot at the preacher, and, shaking off the dust from his shoes against home, neighborhood, community, and native land, go wandering freely and blithely through the world, commanding at a word everything that money can buy. And that is everything except those spiritual values not subject to the cash payment system, but which, by our premise, he has not yet learned to appreciate. This is *individuation*, and in a double sense it is a process of abstraction. In the first place, its instrument is money, the supreme abstraction, pulverizer, and solvent of intimate human relations, of consensus, solidarities, whole situations, configurations, *gestalten*. In the second place, it abstracts the hero, or perhaps the villain, of our drama from his rootage in particular time, place, and social meaning, and sends him circling as an individualistic atom, incredibly abstract and interchangeable with all other such human atoms, through the modern world, where the abstract and interchangeable, impersonal, purchasable social contacts of secondary groups are substituted for the concrete, inviolable, personal, non-purchasable contacts of primary groups. These are, pre-eminently, the family, play group, neighborhood, and religious communion, the last named so fitly called by Josiah Royce "the beloved community."[13]

In an earlier paper I have tried to show that the invention of tools is the foundation of culture. Tools, including symbols as tools of the mind, created a new kind of environment, namely, that of culture itself, and a new kind of inheritance which is the culture heritage. Let us recall again our own definition of culture as whatsoever man (or any other creature) has learned as a member of society, has stored externally by means of tools and symbols, and has transmitted socially as social values with their corresponding personal attitudes. Culture is sometimes more briefly characterized as the mode of life of a people, or in Wissler's phrases the "entire round of life in its individual activities," or "the aggregate thoughts and deeds of the tribe," wherein he takes tribe to mean any group possessing a single culture, even though it be a large modern nation.[14]

In all this, the most interesting thing for the present discussion is Wissler's notion of "the universal pattern" of culture. His theory, as developed in a chapter by that title, is that all tribal cultures, from the simplest to the most highly complex, and in all ages so far as we have any knowledge of them, are built upon one and the same pattern. The pattern itself is made up of great trait complexes which Dr. Wissler lists as follows: 1. speech, 2. material traits, 3. art, 4. mythology and scientific knowledge, 5. religious practices, 6. family and social systems, 7. property, 8. government, 9. war. While he admits that the outline is incomplete and may easily be elaborated, Wissler rightly claims that this general outline will be found to fit all cultures to which one may seek to apply it.[15] . . . .

It is a singular fact that the "entire round of life in its individual activities," everywhere and within all cultures no

---

[13]Cf. Josiah Royce, The Problem of Christianity, Vol. I, p. xxvi, et passim.

[14]Cf. Clark Wissler, Man and Culture (New York, 1923), pp. 48-49.

[15]Ibid., Chap. V, "The Universal Pattern."

matter how divergent, falls under precisely this scheme with
its nine main heads, to which should undoubtedly be added
that artificial stimulation or depression of the nervous systems by means of foods, drinks, smokes, or chewing cuds
which I shall characterize by the single word *dope*. This
seems to be one of the omnipresent trait complexes which
make up the universal culture scheme; and others may yet
be named, although the list of nine, or ten, heads with the
various subheads listed by Wissler will be found surprisingly
accurate and complete.

The relation between Dr. Wissler's "culture scheme" and
his "universal culture pattern" is as follows. All cultures
have language, but some have English, others Persian, others
Chinese, and so on. All cultures possess dwellings, a sub-
trait under the general category called "material traits,"
but some build a snowhouse or igloo, while elsewhere it may
take the form of a skin tent or tipi, a bark-sided long house,
a tree loft, a grass kraal, a timbered Colonial mansion, a
stone chateau, a brick country house, or a stucco bungalow.
Yet every one of these conforms to the underlying scheme
of a constructed dwelling place.

The relation between these two aspects of culture is perfectly exemplified in the technique of weaving. All woven
fabrics, from those using the coarsest reeds to those utilizing the finest gossamer threads of silk, are composed of
warp and woof, which necessarily and unavoidably run at
right angles to each other. Consequently, all designs in
woven fabrics are "stepped" designs, that is, possessing a
contour similar to the profile of a flight of steps on a stair-
case. If they are in reed basketry, the steps are very promi-
nent; but, if the threads are fine and the woof is soft, the
long "pile" or "nap" hides the steps, and the outline flows
in smooth and soft contours, yielding the marvelously
modulated designs or patterns of the finest wall hangings
and rugs.

So it is, likewise, with culture. The universal *scheme* of
culture is the chain or warp of the fabric, while the rich
and unique content that is woven into that scheme is the
characteristic *pattern* of the particular tribal culture. This
distinction is of the utmost significance for our present
discussion, since it involves the possibility of a *world* culture

as the outcome of the present chaotic condition upon this globe. The answer will depend upon one's conception of the nature of culture. Is a culture a homespun and indivisible garment of the folk soul woven by the hand of its own destiny, or is it a universal scheme of standardized and interchangeable parts, a ready-made garment flung together by the profit seekers?

If one follows exclusively the line of thinking developed by those ethnologists who have expanded Wissler's original formulation, he finds himself drifting toward the notion that the several traits of various cultures may, by competition and survival, produce a composite culture which might be conceived as eventually circling the globe and becoming the common possession of all mankind. From such a point of view the expansion of European machine-made products, axes, sewing machines, chewing gum, canned goods, graphophones, Ford cars, and so on, would be hailed as the laying of foundations for the coming world culture. Since any culture is like all other cultures in its general, basic scheme, that is, its warp, and differs only in the particular local form of its pattern expression, namely, in its woof, why cannot the particular pattern that wins in the struggle be substituted by insertion into the warp or scheme which underlies all other cultures, and the whole world thereby become alike in that particular respect? Viewed from our present point of view, it seems to entail no great loss of cultural integrity to thus borrow *patterns*, since the *scheme* remains intact. In other words, the warp threads are unaltered and undisturbed; only the woof is changed, to one of a different color or fullness. The fabric is just as good, and, moreover, it now is more like the other fabrics on the looms of life upon this globe. This seems crude and mechanical; but, when one considers that it applies not only to material traits, but to the highest artistic and ethical values, there comes a vision of humane ideals, emancipation of woman, constitutional government, preventive medicine, labor-saving machines, and universal education circling the earth and weaving themselves into the warp of every culture under the sun. . . . .

Lester F. Ward suggested that beyond "civilization" there might be reached a stage which he called "enlightenment," and characterized by such things as universal education, emancipation of woman, and a social collectivism in which the benefits of invention and discovery would be equitably distributed in the interest of the general welfare. This last he called "the socialization of achievement." . . . .

While agreeing to the fullest extent with the interpretation of civilization as the "most external and artificial" of cultural conditions, a condition brought about, as has been shown in our preceding discussion, by the *machine* and *money* — the latter the prince of abstractions — I am not prepared to accept civilization as the *end*, but would suggest that it may be conceived as the beginning, of a new era. The thesis here offered is that it is simply the universal, interchangeable, aspect of *all* cultures, and that it may hold out to us the key to a new epoch, or, as Spengler himself uses the term, an epoch in itself, in its sense of a "turning-point" or "moment of change,"[16] capable of ushering in a genuine world culture.

The preceding pages have tried to expose the essential nature of the machine as a compound power-driven tool, in its mechanical character, and as an extension of the abstracting tendency in modern social life which dissolves collective solidarities and puts into general circulation the human atom, namely, the free-floating, moneyed, unsocialized individual.

In primitive tribes war is oftentimes a kind of sport and not a very dangerous one at that, because of the crudity of the weapons and the nature of the struggle. This is carried on largely at rather safe distance, with much harmless but ferocious din of tom-toms or war cries, and only occasional hand-to-hand combat. Even among civilized societies until very recently war was not so deadly as we might suppose. King Richard the Lionheart, he of the battle-ax with its fabled twenty pounds of steel, roamed over Europe for many long years hunting trouble. In twenty years he found less of it than a few minutes "over the top" in World War I could have shown him for the asking. For a powerful knight in full armor those encounters of Richard's day were, it would seem, somewhat similar to the modern football scrimmage as viewed by many of us on some frozen Thanksgiving

---

[16]Oswald Spengler, *The Decline of the West* (New York, 1929), Vol. II, p. 33. See translator's footnote.

field in the early days of mass play and tandem line bucking.

Warfare of the Lionheart and football type was quite a personal affair and subject to the limitations of the human personality. Today it is a colossal extension of factory machine methods to impersonal, wholesale destruction. As it unfolds its real nature, every personal aspect of it fades away—without personal grievance, without even knowledge as to *why*, without a voice concerning *how*, without sight of the foe in many cases, without romance or glory—the modern soldier tends to shrink into a mere cog in a vast lethal machine, himself robbed of personality, and the machine itself so devoid of soul that it no longer seeks a foeman worthy of its steel, but makes war indifferently upon armed forces, civilians, women and children, the aged, the sick, and the dying alike, by methods that unfortunately we have no need to describe.

The significant aspect of it all for this present discussion is that the infernal thing has become dehumanized, and more or less completely abstract, inasmuch as the individual units and situations are standardized and interchangeable, without connection between the deed and the actuating motive except through such vague symbols as national causes, war slogans, flags, and military insignia, routine, and authority.

In the case of the gunman and racketeer, the same devastating trail of that serpent, the untamed abstracting machine, lies across the whole scene. In the first place, one beholds high explosives themselves, which, more than anything else in the world except electric control, pulverize concrete human configurations. With its advent the bow became a musket barrel, the arrow shrank into a ball of lead, and the finger trigger replaced the yeoman's strong right arm. All that we gaze upon in horror today is the outcome of that first abstraction which parted the clenched foemen and slipped the lethal machine between them. At first simple, a mere tool, it has added link to link, separating at every step foeman farther from foeman, and motive farther from deed, until the war machines (fatally accurate word!) dominate the world, dehumanize fighting, and, while "belated Goths" prate of the fighting "instinct," warfare is transformed into the complete outraging of every instinct, as the thing misnamed "shell shock" apparently proves.

When this mechanical pattern comes to be allied with vendetta folkways and the criminal drives of unsocialized men, behold the crowning blot upon civilized life, namely, those most dastardly of assassins, the scientifically equipped gangsters, who pursue their sordid feuds in the ruthless slaughter of defenseless victims, their women, or even their children, always operating with *machine* guns of some sort at a safe distance, or from the rear, or by ambush of any kind, but never in fair face-to-face fighting. Then, when even sudden, cowardly ambush seems too risky, we behold the most diabolical abstraction the world has ever seen. That is the well-named "infernal machine," set to explode in the hands of someone the author has never seen, but who stands in his mind purely as a symbol for wrongs actual or imagined. So infernally abstract does the whole thing become that it is treated as a mere incident if any one of a score of innocent and unwitting agents in the postal service or mere bystanders should chance to fall victim to the plot.

I submit that such inhuman, even diabolical, deeds are possible only as the result of the abstracting process working itself out along two lines at the same time. One is mechanical, and eliminates the personal prowess and fair-play aspect from combat itself. The other dissolves human solidarity and moral idealism on its truly social levels, and reduces the human being in such situations to the role of prime mover in a machine-ridden process, but a prime mover merely in the mechanical sense, with no more of moral dignity than the machine which he sets in motion.

TECHNOCRACY AND SOCIAL ENGINEERING*

THE WORD "TECHNOCRACY" has suddenly become a symbol for the hopes of destitute millions and the fears of a multitude of others more fortunately situated. It may not be out of place, therefore, to suggest that during the course of all this vast public discussion three, and only three, major propositions actually have been made, whether by the "technocrats" themselves or by their official, or self-appointed, expounders.

Of these the first is purely a matter of engineering, and declares that the modern machine technique is piling the land high with mountains of goods at the very same time that it is forcing more and more millions of men permanently out of work and into hopeless poverty and distress. The second proposition asserts that the machine economy can no longer be run by means of a price system, which is a matter of debatable economic theory. The third suggests that technologists should be given control of the economic and social order, and this is a problem that most concerns sociology and political science. These three propositions, falling respectively within the fields of technological engineering, economic theory, and social politics, are all that have been really put forward; and, if we were able now to discuss them adequately, we should have the essence of "technocracy" as promulgated thus far. The limits of time will admit, however, of only a very partial treatment in these remarks.

1. The first of these propositions is purely a matter of engineering in the technological sense as commonly understood. That is to say, it deals with the physicochemical materials and forces of nature, along lines which only an engineer is qualified to question. The rest of us, maintaining that modesty which befits the layman, must take the word of the engineers on this subject as final, and reason from it as from an established premise. Let us notice how the technologists have stated it:

---

*Presidential address delivered before the Pacific Sociological Society at Whittier College, January 14, 1933.

For the first time in history, as a result of the technological advance, we have achieved an economy of plenty in the midst of a hodgepodge of debt and unemployment. The plain fact is that the machine and men cannot both work on a parity basis any longer. The machine has pushed man out of work. There isn't room for him any more.[1]

Thus runs the bare proposition; they elaborate it as follows:

. . .the high-water mark of industrial employment in America was reached in 1918, and ever since that time, through all the great years of the boom, it has been steadily falling. As industry becomes more and more mechanized one door after another has been shut to human labor. And all the while the Midas profit is put to producing more goods. In the end one sees the producers, fewer and fewer in numbers, engulfed in goods which they can neither sell nor use, bowed down with interest and dividend-debts which they cannot pay. Beside them is the little concentrated band of owners, swamped in money for which there is no use. Opposed to them is a vast army, laborers, white-collars, professionals, and all with neither food nor clothing nor money to pay for them. Spread out before all three is the spectacle of a gutted continent, its resources wasted and flung away in the crazy race for the profit that strangled the system.[2]

All are familiar with the details of the picture so vividly painted by these technologists. They have shown us really appalling processes at work crowding the laborer out at a constantly accelerating speed. Where it took seventy hours for a man to produce a ton of steel in 1900, it required only thirteen man-hours in 1929, and a similar reduction of the human labor factor is shown all along the line.

The social tragedy that follows from it all is that machines cannot eat food, wear clothing, ride in automobiles, or read books. Only human beings are constituted to consume these products, and since they have no work they cannot get possession of the vast "surplus," sardonically so-called, but must go hungering, shivering, begging, or plundering; eking out a wretched existence, while the huge product of the machine continues to pile up in the warehouses of the futile and baffled owners. The "technocrats" point this out, and say it will grow steadily worse. "At the present downward rate," they predict, "we will have 25,000,000 unem-

[1]Wayne W. Parish, "Technocracy's Question," *New Outlook*, 161:13-17, December, 1932.

[2]"Technology Smashes the Price System" (prepared by Howard Scott), *Harper's Monthly Magazine*, 166:129-42, January, 1933.

ployed by 1934, without taking into account any acceleration from disorder."[3]

The mind shudders at the prospect before the world unless something can be done to lay the axe to the root of the trouble. Technocracy has, however, little new to offer on this particular point except impressive examples, since the so-called overproduction and its cause in low wages have long been known. The technocrats made in the same connection, nevertheless, a contribution which in itself amounts to the most tremendous challenge to our collective intelligence and social idealism it is possible to imagine. I refer to their further assertion that "with what is known of technology today in this country, it is now necessary for the adult population, ages 25 to 45, to work but 660 hours per year per individual to produce a standard of living for the entire population ten times above the average income of 1929."[4] Or, as some writers have put it, the delivery of four hours' labor two days a week by the said adults "would be enough to run the country, on the basis of our present equipment, so as to give every family in America the equivalent of an annual income of $20,000."[5]

If the half of this be true, it takes the ground away from the economic doctrine that the niggardliness of nature and the comparative unproductiveness of man make long toil and low income the inevitable lot of the masses of mankind despite the utmost possibilities of economic justice and social idealism. That sort of teaching is henceforth as outworn and impossible as the system which saw its birth. The supremely significant service of the technocrats, as of the magazines and newspapers which have disseminated it among the public, lies just at this point. Even if nothing else that technocracy has said should prove important in the end, the very act of making these facts known has let the cat out of the bag once for all. Henceforth, we reason no more from the premise of an economic deficit and a "pain economy," but from the exact opposite. If these statements of the technologists are correct, as they doubtless are in sub-

---

[3]Parish, *op. cit.*, p. 17.

[4]*Ibid.*, p. 13.

[5]Jefferson Chase, "Wanted: an American N.E.P.," *Vanity Fair*, December, 1932, p. 72.

stance, the only obstacle to general social welfare will be the lack of sufficient social intelligence and democratic idealism to bring it to pass. Long faces and lugubrious talk about these technocratic revelations are a reflection upon our humanity and love of social justice. Hearing such things we, the whole of America, should hail the day of man's deliverance from the unremitting and poorly rewarded toil of the relatively unproductive past. An exponent of technocracy puts it well: "Instead of being a cause for remorse," he remarks, "this should be the most joyful proclamation in history. Let the machine do man's work for him. Let him have leisure."

2. The second major assertion of the technocrats is that the "price system" will no longer work under the system of production which the enormous expansion of machinery has forced upon the Western world. On this point we shall have little to say. They actually seem to be talking against the system of wages and profits, although they constantly direct their remarks against the "price" system in particular, as the pivot of the present system of distribution. This is immensely significant, but it is a problem to be threshed out by economists and financial experts.

3. The third, and the only other, major proposition accredited to technocracy is of very doubtful origin, although there can be little doubt about its absurdity. It seems to suggest that the affairs of this nation should be turned over to the technologists, leaving them to run the affairs by the same methods with which their remarkable successes in technical engineering have been attained. That mysterious word "technocracy" seems to mean for many persons simply this rule of the technologists. It may have been meant to convey that sense, but it might also mean simply the rule of technological considerations, principles, and laws. If it is the latter that is intended, it is already hoary with years, having been enunciated in Karl Marx's theory of the economic interpretation of history, and in other words by various social scientists of later date.

If, on the other hand, the technocrats really mean to hint that national affairs should be placed in their hands, they are the victims of an absurd conceit, which proceeds from a tendency to confuse technological and social engineering. Engineering in the technological sense has to do with the manipulation of the materials and forces of inanimate nature. Social engineering attempts to modify or direct the basic wishes and acquired social attitudes of human beings as members of society. These personality traits, as engineers will find, are much less clearly understood and immensely more obstinate than even the native granite or casehardened steel over which they have won the mastery. President Hoover himself found it much easier to harness and divert the mighty current of the Colorado River than to bring the people of the adjoining states into harmonious cooperation with the project. "Technocrats" who covertly or openly aspire to taking over the direction of the life of this nation in the name of technological efficiency are simply displaying the valor of ignorance in the social field. The tremendous emotional forces already aroused both for and against their pronouncements should serve to show them that the inauguration of the technocratic scheme, or any other program of social reform or economic readjustment, involves the control of social forces concerning which all their brilliant engineering experience in itself yields them not the slightest understanding. Whatever they may know, and it is a good deal in the case of some of them, about the modification of human behavior, they learned as men and as citizens, or as students of social science, but not as engineers in the technological sense.

The problem is one of consciously directing social change along lines of general welfare and social progress. This is a problem which sociologists of the last one hundred years have earnestly studied but with almost completely negative results. We now begin to know how to state the problem of social progress, but practically nothing about the social technique required to bring it to solution.

Perhaps sociologists will be found most reluctant about rushing into the breach just here, simply because they have studied, during a hundred years, the problem which the most self-confident workers in other fields seem quite keen to solve out of hand, although hardly prepared to state it clearly.

Without overlooking for a moment the immense complexity and baffling stubbornness of social forces, it does seem warranted to say that the immense productivity of applied physical science and machinery forces upon us the task of diverting a larger share of the national income into the hands of masses of men and women who are its natural and rightful consumers. Since they are not now working, and hence not drawing wages at all, the immediate task is to transfer goods from those who own but cannot consume them, to those who must consume but do not own them. This will, inevitably, have to be done, and it is possible to think of only three ways by which it can be accomplished. The first is to transfer it to them through jobs of some kind or other; the second is to dispense it by doles of some sort; the third is to leave them to drift about empty handed until in sheer desperation they rise up and seize it. The last-named alternative spells the worst of calamities for all concerned, but there are other possibilities only less ominous. By attempting to evade this momentous issue, fiddling while Rome burns, it is not absolutely impossible, although scarcely believable, that America should yet fall victim to the rule of the so-called "Man on Horseback," or the domination of a revolutionary conflict class, called frankly the "dictatorship of the proletariat."

One way of escaping both those catastrophes might be for this nation to proceed to dictate to itself, after the manner in which a person of purpose and character dictates to himself. It can be done in either case only by planning instead of drifting, and by subordinating the more fleeting and partial impulses to that larger and more permanent interest represented by a deliberately formulated and consciously willed purpose or goal. The fact that social groups, especially the vast national ones, blunder along in the blind, self-defeating ways of the amoeba or other low forms of life has been familiar to sociologists from the days of Herbert Spencer. We speak much of progress and societal self-direction, but history shows very little, if any, of either. The principal reason for this would seem to lie in the lack of a deliberating, planning organ, even in the case of the most highly civilized societies. Yet there seems to be no way out of the present predicament except through the guidance and virtual dictation of some more highly centralized and authoritative directing body than now exists.

The forms of democratic government in the more direct

sense have failed in this country, although, as some have ably argued, the essential urge toward democracy has not necessarily diminished. It might be saved through some plan for centralizing responsibility in a comparatively small number of persons exercising large powers, subject to recall but otherwise set free from popular clamor. In the very act of seeming to abandon it, genuine self-government might thus be made more effective and secure. Not even politically immobile America can hope to blunder along much further in the face of millions growing daily more destitute and more desperate. While a simple rural civilization can usually muddle through, the modern machine-driven world economy can no longer be endured under a policy of aimless drift. The acute human situation now facing us calls for far-sighted and disinterested planning such as can never be achieved by means of the shortsighted, selfish policies of pressure politics. One of the greatest and most urgent tasks of our times is to invent some way of placing a much larger share of societal self-direction into the hands of the wisest and best. It seems not only theoretically reasonable but practically imperative that a nation claiming high enlightenment should take steps toward exercising some of that same planful foresight which is recognized as the attribute of superior men in the ordering of their own personal affairs. The idea here in mind goes beyond currently proposed economic councils and boards of strategy, excellent as they are, in the fact that social and cultural values wider than engineering techniques or economic interests in the narrow sense are regarded as of equal or even greater importance. At any rate, that community, whether county, state, or national, which first succeeds in deliberately planning the social and economic life for the general welfare will be humanity's pioneer in social engineering.*

*Reprinted from *Sociology and Social Research*, 17:331-39, March-April, 1933.

TOWARD GESTALT SOCIOLOGY

IN THESE TIMES that "old cast-iron universe," whose joints William James endeavored to loosen up a bit in order "to leave a little room for personal faith," is beginning to show more vulnerable spots than Achilles. While we have not exactly taken it by the heels, it begins to look as if the man of intellectual profession might once more dare to call his soul his own.

The works of Professor Eddington will of course have to be evaluated by those equipped with the conceptual technique of mathematical physics and metaphysics, but the general drift of it for a philosophy of life can be sensed even by a wayfaring man, though a fool, or a sociologist. The layman more fully realizes the utter abstractness and complete universality of pure science when he reads that in certain physical experiments the observer cannot distinguish past from future, earlier from later. "Time's arrow" has ceased to fly, and the only clue to the future is to follow the trail toward "entropy," which means that "random element which can increase in the universe but can never decrease."[1] . . . . [A lengthy omission at this point consists of preliminary statements regarding some of the scientific bases of a *gestalt* sociology.]

When the *person* appears, we are confronted with a new situation, and if one considers that the person possesses both social status and social values it becomes plain that the situation is an irreducibly complicated one. No departmental game of "pass the button" can meet the methodological problem presented to the social sciences. Following Allport, students in this field may go "below" into psychology for explanatory principles, or even, with Spencer, delve deeper still, into biology. But such procedure is really a form of *abstraction*, inasmuch as the investigator draws away from the actual situation that he started out to study. He finds an explanation, but it is the explanation of something else, and something, moreover, not really present. An explanation in psychological terms of the *individual*, even

---

[1] A. S. Eddington, *The Nature of the Physical World* (Cambridge University, 1928), pp. 74, 99, *et passim*.

the interacting *individual* if there is any such thing, is not an explanation of the *person,* inseparably intertwined with his *group* and its *culture.* This is the total, or whole, situation that confronts the sociologist. One may turn away from it and seek a neat psychological explanation. The more strictly psychological it becomes, the more universal its application and the less it elucidates the concrete and total situation presented by society. As with Alice in Wonderland, the cat has faded away and left only its smile when one starts out to know a culture group and ends with only a psychological explanation of it.

The rejoinder may be that Professor Allport does not advocate recourse to general but to social psychology, which by his own definition deals with the *interacting* individuals of the social group. This is good as far as it goes, but does it go far enough? The question is whether the thing we call "society" is not such a total situation, such a *gestalt* or configuration, such an actual and vitally functioning whole, that it must be understood *as such,* and upon its own *level* as a genuine emergent, without constantly running back to touch home base in psychology or any other discipline developed through the investigation of a single aspect of the whole, no matter how important, as all will allow the interacting individual, as one aspect, to be. . . . .

Now in Allport's "explanation" by recourse to psychology do we fall back upon a position from which the social behavior can be foretold with any greater success than upon the social or culture-group level? If so, it would be a very vague and general form of prediction, because knowledge that men will be driven by certain "prepotent reflexes" or any other psychophysical drives is a very poor guide to the foretelling of the social and cultural forms that these will assume in a given social situation. And the more truly the life of the culture group represents a real emergent, the more helpless and irrelevant the psychological explanation in terms of the individual becomes.

Do not these considerations permit us to raise the question whether the theories of emergent evolution and *gestalt* psychology do not suggest that a method adequate to their object matter remains yet to be worked out by the social sciences? At any rate, it is interesting to note that the social psychologists themselves have taken the first steps in that direction. Six years ago, in her book, *Creative Experience*, Mary Parker Follett argued: "As we have found that a sensation never exists in experience but is a psychological abstraction, that a "trait" of personality is also a psychological abstraction, so many times our studies reveal to us that the meaning of a social situation is to be found not in its elements viewed separately but only in the total situation, or to use the still more suggestive word of the *Gestalt* school, a *Gesammtsituation*."[2] She goes on to say that "it must be remembered that the *Gesammtsituation* cannot be comprehended by thinking of it as a matter of mere interaction." The key to genuine understanding Miss Follett sees in the principle of "integration," which Professor Kimball Young developed earlier in relation to *personality*."[3]

Professor Watson, according to Miss Follett, had declared in 1919 that "the behaviorist is interested in integrations and total activities of the *individual*."[4] Social psychologists like herself and Kimball Young are interested in the total situations and integration of *personality*. Should not sociologists be equally interested in the total situation that has been called "society"? It includes at least the person, and the culture, and the *togetherness* of the persons and their culture (including personal attitudes and social values), all together constituting a *whole* which we should perhaps call the *culture group,* to distinguish it from those cultureless groups of other beings which are nevertheless societies.

The historical school of American ethnologists, notably Professor Lowie and Professor Kroeber, has taken the lead in this direction, as the reader of the current literature in both ethnology and sociology is well aware.[5] The extreme expression of that method in the interpretative principle, "All culture from culture," is doubtless overstated, but its stimulating and far-reaching influence on the social sciences

---

[2]Mary P. Follett, *Creative Experience* (New York, 1924), p. 113.

[3]Kimball Young, *Source Book for Social Psychology* (New York, 1927), p. 207.

[4]Italics mine.

[5]*Cf.* especially, Robert H. Lowie, *Culture and Ethnology* (New York, 1917); and A. L. Kroeber, "The Super-Organic," *American Anthropologist*, XIX (April-June, 1917). Also articles in sociological and anthropological journals.

is a fine demonstration of the reward that comes from fearless examination of culture as a total situation existing on its own level.

Let us take a lesson from a neighboring field. Thus, in *Gestalt Psychology*, Professor Köhler shows minutely how "the organism reacts to an actual *constellation* of stimuli by a total process which, as a functional whole, is the response to the whole situation."[6] In this we see a repudiation of the abstracting, atomizing procedure of the older sensationalist and associational psychology. Have we not reached a place in sociology where a larger grasp of the whole social configuration is to be sought after and welcomed? One finds the biologist C. Lloyd Morgan also speaking in that same *gestalt* terminology: "According to the evidence" . . . he remarks, "color lives *in the whole situation;* in other words, it has being in virtue of the extrinsic relatedness of person (body-mind) and thing. . . ."[7]

As for our own sociological "whole situation," there is a rich world of attitudes and values that exists essentially as a total situation whose phenomena have being only by virtue of the extrinsic relatedness of persons, group, and culture. Consequently, there is required what one might call a *personal-group-history* method for the purpose of dealing with it. In such a total situation one can no more abstract from either the personal, or the groupal, or the cultural aspect and expect to understand the "society" than he can pull out either the warp or the woof of a piece of cloth and find the fabric itself left. Human social life is a seamless web, in which the personal life-histories of its members form the woof, interwoven in rich complexity of attitude-value pattern with the cultural traditions that constitute the warp. Professor Cooley's suggestion for the study of juvenile delinquency through the consideration of the life histories of one hundred delinquent boys is an example of this method, while his "organic view" of life is a recognition of the significance of the "whole situation," as opposed to single aspects, as a general principle or method of social research.

---

[6]Wolfgang Köhler, *Gestalt Psychology* (New York, 1929), p. 106.

[7]C. Lloyd Morgan, *Emergent Evolution* (London, 1923), p. 229.

We have noted above the fact that behaviorism in psychology very early expressed an interest in the "total activities of the individual," but there are found those among psychologists who do not think that it has succeeded in doing so. On the contrary, so eminent an authority as Köhler seems to think that the behavioristic approach is so narrowly circumscribed that it attributes to mental phenomena a barrenness that is the antithesis of their richness as functioning wholes. In its exclusive preoccupation with the two concepts of positive and negative conditioning the behavioristic method, as Köhler sees it, so impoverishes the object matter that upon comparison with the world of the physicist "you will find that even physical systems are by far richer in the variety of their kinds of function than is the nervous system of man in the eyes of a radical behaviorist. A soapbubble does not show us reflexes, it is true; therefore, we cannot expect to find conditioned reflexes in it. Nevertheless, those functional properties which the soap-bubble does exhibit are decidedly superior in some respects to the monotony of reflexes and conditioned reflexes."[8]

This formidable opponent of behaviorism attributes the "astounding sterility" of the latter in developing productive concepts to a dogmatism so pronounced that one is given to understand that "the truth was revealed to them in its perfection at the birth of behavioristic psychology. . . 'Thou shalt not acknowledge direct experience in science' is the first commandment, and 'Thou shalt not conceive of other functions but reflexes and conditioned reflexes' is the second."[9]

Of these dogmas, if we may so designate them, the first will concern us later in this discussion, but the second bears directly upon the present issue.

Köhler's indictment, like the inimitable *reductio ad absurdum* by Professor Faris,[10] may seem a bit hard on the behaviorists; but, since tough-mindedness is one of their special roles, we need not concern ourselves about that. The important consideration just now is that here we seem to see a psychological movement that started out with an

[8]*Cf.* Köhler, *op. cit.*, pp. 55-56.
[9]*Loc. cit.*
[10]Ellsworth Faris, "The Subjective Aspect of Culture," in *Publications of the American Sociological Society*, 19:37-46.

expressed interest in "total activities" and ended, if Köhler and other critics are correct, in a point of view notorious for its arbitrary narrowness.

If such is really the fate of behaviorism it is the outcome of a fundamental flaw in the underlying method with which it set out. Professor Watson has ably illustrated and defended his point of view in various writings,[11] holding, as I understand it, that it aims to be nothing more than a method. Concentrating upon objective and physically observable reactions of the individual, it vastly simplifies its problem by ignoring the introspective, subjective aspect of the behavior patterns. But eventually that which was merely ignored comes, with some extremists at least, to be denied, practically if not in theory. Thus that which began, contrary to its own expressed intention, as an abstraction, ends as an "ism," in fact as well as in the name itself. For behaviorism really is an *abstraction* exactly after the fashion of the classical economics of Adam Smith and his followers. Both start out by a gross oversimplification of their object of investigation. Economics, by assuming that all human actions are dictated by egoism and self-interest, created the myth of the "economic man," and in so doing presented what Vaihinger calls "a standard example" of the "abstractive" or "neglective" fiction.[12]

Behaviorism in its turn adopted a similar fiction, also for methodological purposes, namely, the abstractive fiction of neglecting conscious experience, which is, to be sure, the most difficult aspect of personality to handle, but also the most important. Both classical economics and behavioristic psychology, by taking the easier road in the interest of method, sold the right to serve as an adequate interpretation of their object matter, and reduced themselves to a fundamental inadequacy despite their many contributions in a smaller way.

Turning now to the former of the two behavioristic "commandments," as formulated by Köhler, namely, the taboo against acknowledging "direct experience" in science, we

[11]John B. Watson, *Psychology from the Standpoint of a Behaviorist*, and *The Ways of Behaviorism* (Philadelphia and London, 1919).

[12]Hans Vaihinger, *The Philosophy of "As If"* (C. K. Ogden's translation; London and New York, 1924), p. 19.

are faced with another issue of importance for sociological interpretation. The pronounced tendency of this behavioristic canon to invade sociological thinking and to build up a sort of sociological behaviorism is well known to those familiar with current discussion in our field. In a few moments we shall have to consider the tendency more in detail, but let us first notice the issue in its larger aspect.

In face of the predilection of many persons for a materialistic and mechanistic account of all things, it is significant to hear Professor Lloyd Morgan say, "I shall have occasion hereafter to urge, as against radical behaviorists, that mental guidance of events counts for progress and betokens a kind of relatedness that is effective."[13] In a later passage, he has the courage, after acknowledging a physical world which is "beyond proof," to add: "I acknowledge also God, Who is, I contend, beyond disproof."[14] After asserting further that "ideals of value" are also real in the fullest naturalistic sense under the rubric of relatedness at their own emergent level, he posits an *Activity*, as "omnipresent throughout" the natural world, and suggests that the avenue of approach toward it "in each one of us must be sought in some kind of immediate acquaintance within the current changes of one's own psychical system."[15]

The significant phrase in that is its reference to "immediate acquaintance," wherein an eminent scientist sounds not only a religious but even a mystical note. For the other, scarcely less remarkable, admission respecting mental causation, Morgan enjoys the support of Professor Jennings, who boldly declares: "Emergent evolution so does away with that monstrous absurdity that has so long been a reproach to biological science; the doctrine that ideas, ideals, purposes have no effect on behavior. The mental determines what happens as does any other determiner."[16] The assertion that it does not is, according to Professor Jennings, a purely *a priori* notion, with "no ground based on experimental analysis." This, from a biologist eminent among experimentalists, one sees supported by a physicist,

---

[13]Morgan, *op. cit.*, p. 20.

[14]*Ibid.*, pp. 61-62.

[15]*Ibid.*, pp. 207-9.

[16]*Loc. cit.*

likewise famed for experimental research, when Professor
Compton finds in his exploration of the physical world room
for "a certain freedom of choice" and the corollary that
"one's thoughts are not the result of molecular reactions
obeying fixed physical laws."[17]

This brings us to an issue which is of major importance
to the theme of the present paper, and that is the question as to what kinds of evidence sociologists are going to
welcome in their effort to understand social phenomena.
Professor Köhler, in discussing certain problems of psychology aroused by the organism's total response to a
constellation of stimuli, uses a happy and significant phrase
when, as one way out of the psychologist's dilemma, he
suggests a determination to *"trust all kinds of experience
impartially."*[18] Whatever may be the response of psychologists to such a challenge, does it call for a scientific and
philosophical catholicity that sociologists are prepared to
exercise at this stage? As I take it, Professor Hornell Hart
was pleading for intellectual hospitality of that sort in his
paper on "Mana, Magic, and Animism in Modern Religion,"
read before the American Sociological Society at its last
annual session.[19] In the haste and confusion of such a huge
gathering this issue was not squarely met, but it would be
interesting to know what the response of the sociological
fraternity at large would be.

No one needs to be told that sociology has been shifting
its center of interest overwhelmingly toward research, and
the development of the technique of research, for the last
decade at least. In so doing the influence of physical science and its method has been almost everywhere dominant,
with consequent emphasis upon minute analysis, quantitative
measurement, and statistical manipulation. To a large degree
these procedures have been taken over from psychology;
but, since that science has become, in some of its aspects,
almost a division of physics, it amounts to the same thing
in the end. For this reason the trenchant criticisms directed
against current psychology by Köhler will be found equally

---

[17]Arthur Compton, "Science's New View of Evolution," *Literary
Digest*, Vol. 105, June 21, 1930, p. 16; quoted from *New York Times*.
[18]Köhler, *op. cit.*, pp. 106-7.
[19]At Washington, D.C., December, 1929.

true and timely if applied to sociology without the change
of a single word. "If we wish to imitate the physical sciences, we must not imitate them in their contemporary,
most developed form; we must imitate them in their historical youth, when their state of development was comparable to our own at the present time. Otherwise, we
should behave like boys who try to copy the imposing manners of full-grown men without understanding their *raison
d'etre*, also without seeing that in development one cannot
jump over intermediate and preliminary phases. . . . Let
us imitate the natural sciences, but intelligently!"[20]

In the early stages of any science certainly, and perhaps
during all of its history except the latest stage, qualitative
observation will vastly overshadow quantitative measurement. Indeed the qualitative procedure is the necessary pre-
condition of the measuring method, and it alone can give
the investigator an intelligent notion as to what he is measuring and why he measures it. Now it would be not only
ungracious but narrow minded to withhold hearty approval
of the many fine pieces of social research that have piled
up to the credit of this more recent sociological movement.
Moreover, the attitude behind it is indispensable for the
continued progress of the social sciences. Yet at the same
time, who has failed to note that we are producing all too
many "projects" that not only shed no light on the "sociohistorical actuality" but betray themselves as nothing but
an occasion for statistical acrobatics? One recalls a wise
graduate dean's remark, that a "doctoral dissertation is
supposed to be a contribution, but usually turns out to be
an exercise."

Referring to what he regards as Fechner's premature
attempt to found experimental psychology by "copying adult
physics," Köhler remarks that Fechner "seems to have been
convinced that measuring in itself would make a science
out of psychology." Psychology did indeed arise about that
time, but according to Köhler it could do so only because
the necessary qualitative knowledge had accumulated, in
various ways, to serve as a basis, upon which the science
arose "rather casually." But in consequence of the un-

---

[20]Köhler, *op. cit.*, pp. 42-44.

critical disposition to copy the quantitative methods of mature physics, we have in consequence, within psychological and especially educational circles, a situation where "hundreds of thousands of quantitative psychophysical experiments have been made almost in vain, because no one knew just what he was measuring or what were the processes upon which the whole procedure was built."[21]   The reader who will note the broken-down research projects that are left strewn along the critical trail of Sorokin in *Contemporary Sociological Theories,* or Thomas in *The Child in America,* will be impressed with the truth of this statement.

There are two tendencies in the human mind, present in varying balance in all persons, and expressing themselves in the great intellectual organizations called arts, sciences, and philosophies.   One disposition or tendency is to split phenomena up into smaller and smaller units in order to observe, compare, and measure more minutely and more exactly.   This is the procedure called *science,* and it yields a vast amount of definite and useful knowledge, but leaves us a dissected and raveled-out world.   For this reason its steady advance has oftentimes made for an illumination of the intellect and a darkening of the spirit in modern times. Men asked science for bread and it gave them bread, although the bread often proved virtually a stone.

While many have thus come to heavy-hearted grief in their philosophy of life, a vast multitude have not.   The reason is that there is an equally persistent tendency in man to build knowledge and dreams into wholes and to live in the presence and shelter of them.   These are the great synthetic creations of art, philosophy, and religion. Each of these moves from diversity toward an inclusive unity.   In the works of *art* we attain the esthetic unity of a single symphony, poem, painting, or temple; a single thing of beauty that is grasped as a whole if grasped at all. In *philosophy* the unifying power inheres in a few comprehensive and logically related concepts which marshal in vast perspective a multitude of facts and ideas. By means of *religion* another great synthesis is attained, drawing upon both art (in ritual) and philosophy (as theology), and

---

[21] *Ibid.,* p. 46.

producing, with the support of both intellect and emotion, a sense of unification of the will of the worshiper with the absolute will. While the remorseless analytical probing and dissecting of the scientific tendency has driven some to cynicism and despair, these great synthesizing movements, within the same culture and the same persons, have renewed in men the will and the joy to live. Neither of these drives, the one toward analysis, the other toward synthesis, has been or will be completely crowded out by the other, because both, as I see it, are permanent, as perpetually recurring phases of every normal and developed personality.

Art, philosophy, and religion are thus equally valid along with science in the pragmatic sense that they help men to live. Perhaps no one would dispute this, but are we ready to go further and say that they are also all equally valid as sources of truth concerning life and the world? The answer, I suppose, will be governed by the degree of naïve and unquestioning credence one places in those "pointer-readings" on a dial which physical science wrings from that "world of shadows" about which A. S. Eddington has spoken. Moreover, one's position will be further affected by his philosophy of nature, particularly whether he is living in a world where unvarying mechanical forces pursue their predetermined course along the path of unilinear evolution, or in the less determined, creative, more free, surprising and spiritual world of emergent and even creative evolution.

If sociology, applying behavioristic methods, elects to stress only the objective and measurable phenomena, it will share the fate of its mentor, in that, while always hard on the trail, and a master of footprints, it may never catch up with the quarry. In so far as this comes true it may be explained by the fact that while living forms occupy *space*, *life* itself, as experience, does not, but endures through *time*. Using these terms in a somewhat common-sense way, I think it is true that the real zest and tang of personal and group life inhere in what we call "experience." Experience, as I am using the term, means the events that a living being goes through in the course of time, insofar as these are stored up in memory and elaborated by consciousness into personal purposes and social values. "Meaning" in this subjective, conscious, purposeful sense is the central fact in the life of the individual, the person, and the group. This being true, what are the implications for sociological method?

For one thing, it implies that the sociological student will have to "trust all kinds of experience, impartially," and that includes subjective experience. A bent for "measuring," as contrasted with evaluating in the qualitative sense, naturally leads to emphasis upon physical aspects because they alone are spatial. But the meaning and significance lie not in the spatial, but in the time dimension. If we try to "measure" time we end with the intervals marked off on a clockface, as Bergson, I believe, points out. The projected time interval has to be measured as a space interval, in other words not measured at all, in its essential aspect of *experience*. Here again we get pointer readings on a dial, but not much of the meaning of true duration is registered by the clock.

I am aware that those competent in that field are saying that the older contrast between space and time is robbed of validity by the discoveries of Einstein and others respecting relativity, the two being merged into "space-time." But I make no pretension to more than a common-sense use of the words here.

It is not only in the field of physics and philosophy that one runs the risk of mistake. In the sociological field also things are not always what they seem at first glance. This is exemplified in the case of three methodological concepts, the first two of these just now much used in social research, namely, "social distance," "human ecology," and "sociology of religion." Let us examine each of these from the present point of view, in order to see whether in these instances research is being directed toward the spatial externals or the essential meaning of collective life.

In social distance we have an expression that is spatial, in its substantive term, more completely than any other word used by sociologists, if we except certain ecological terminology. Yet those who have done most to define, refine, and measure it—as Simmel, Park, and Bogardus—agree in using the term to signify not extent of separation in space (although it may take the form of physical withdrawal at times), but degree of understanding and sympathy between persons. It is therefore, as Professor Hayes remarked,[22] a figurative term, which renders it none the less usual, to say the least.

In this case, while the language of physical relation and measurement is used, and very effectively, we see that it is in its essence an effort to gauge and register the form and degree of certain kinds of personal and group *experience*.

The ecological movement in sociology might seem at first glance to be a dubious attempt at social physics, with its spatially flavored concepts of concentration, centralization, segregation, natural areas, and regional aspects in general. Preoccupation with such things might be expected to lead the sociologist into an abstracting, analyzing dissection of the physical forms of community existence, in a kind of sociological behaviorism that would possibly obscure the real meaning of the life lived through them. Yet, on the contrary, we find Professor House showing[23] how the whole tendency from Brunhes through Mackenzie to Mukerjee has been quite the reverse of atomistic. On the contrary, it has aimed at an intensive study of *concrete wholes* of human life with much of that attention to the "total situation" which I venture to call *gestalt* sociology.

In the field of the sociology of religion we see the significance of a method that seeks to comprehend the entire configuration, especially upon its subjective side. Otherwise, one returns with empty shells of behavior patterns from which the vital meaning has vanished, as at an alien touch. So true is this in the present instance that, if the ecological and statistical approaches are the only ones available, no true sociology of religion need be expected. In directing some student researches in this field at The University of Southern California I have been impressed with the necessity of the method which Professor Lindeman happily styled "the participant observer."[24] Experience in this field, however, suggests the need of something even more intimate which might be called the method of

---

[22]Edward C. Hayes, "Representative Concepts in Sociology," *Sociology and Social Research*, 12:12-17, September-October, 1927.

[23]Floyd N. House, *The Range of Social Theory* (New York, 1929), Chap. VI, "Natural Areas and Territorial Groups."

[24]*Cf.* Eduard C. Lindeman, *Social Discovery* (New York, 1924).

the observing participant. In a word, no one really knows what the attitudes and values of a religious fellowship or communion actually are until he senses their *meaning,* and he can get the full tang and pungency of that only by participation, either with the aid of the "sympathetic imagination" of Cooley, which serves as an incentive in the case of the participant observer, or by dependence upon the scientific detachment and criticism of a cooperating research group, which provides the necessary corrective in the case of the observing but naturally biased participant. Let us illustrate this by reference to a recent study that has attracted much favorable attention.

In their study of "Middletown," as a typical American community,[25] Robert and Helen Lynd have applied the objective, ethnological approach, through description of culture patterns, with notable success. Yet to one whose early life was spent in a neighboring community identical in character, and enjoying active participation in its religious life, their vivid portrayal of the behavioristic side of the Sunday School, prayer meeting, and other gatherings in the churches there struck me as empty and misleading, just because it so perfectly described simply the religious activities from their outer and relatively meaningless side.

Happily the authors themselves realized this and fitly remark:

> These bald statements, set down as accurate descriptions of what a person going to church and Sunday School in Middletown sees and hears, cannot adequately represent the all-important consideration of what these services mean to the Middletown people themselves.[26]

This recognized failure of the objective culture-pattern method to interpret the religious group presents a foretaste of the barrenness that may be expected from such a sociological behaviorism as might conceivably develop if certain tendencies now working should gain the ascendancy. Not as a substitute, but as a correlate, I suggest *gestalt* sociology, among whose characteristics may be named the following:

It will bear in mind the essentially symbolic and abstract unreality of the formulations of even the most exact sciences.

---

[25]Robert S. Lynd and Helen Merrell Lynd, *Middletown: A Study in Contemporary American Culture* (New York, 1929).
[26]*Ibid.,* p. 390.

Mechanistic determinism will not remain a sacred tenet of its philosophy, and it will have room for the surprising freshness of conception that characterizes the theories of emergent evolution. As corollaries to this, *gestalt* sociology will set out boldly to describe and explain the life of human culture groups as presenting a new and autonomous level of phenomena. In so doing it will avoid the abstracting fictions of behaviorism and endeavor to grasp the total situation, the complete configuration of human society. Using where helpful the spatial concepts and measurements of physical science and human ecology, it will go above and beyond them into the study of experience in the subjective conscious sense of meaning and values. This will require it to trust all kinds of experience impartially. What is lost in mathematical exactness may thus be more than made up in sociological insight. There will be analysis in all its work, but still more of synthesis in the end.

Perhaps the reason why artists and poets have often the profounder insight, as compared with scientists and even philosophers, is that they "see life steadily, and see it whole."*

*Reprinted from *Sociology and Social Research*, 15:3-27, September-October, 1930.

BEYOND CIVILIZATION*

UNDER THE INFLUENCE of machine-equipped science, as the present writer has tried to show in another place,[1] life in the West has moved so persistently along the path of analysis and abstraction that machine production, planless distribution, social disorganization, and moral disintegration now seriously imperil the world. In this plight one may agree with Spengler in his *The Decline of the West* that there is possible no turning back through discarding the machine, without accepting his other dictum, that there is no going forward. The watchword, however, must not be merely, Toward Civilization! as in the symposium edited by Professor Charles A. Beard under that title, but Beyond Civilization! As used in this paper, civilization means simply any machine-equipped and machine-ridden culture.

This calls for something more than a slogan—something as definite as our painful ignorance of both fact and truth will permit. It raises the most difficult but most important problem in social science, namely, whether it is possible for society to direct its own course through the application of human intelligence. The outstanding figure here is Lester F. Ward, who devoted his numerous sociological writings to the elucidation of "social telesis," as he chose to call it. The question was formulated most impressively from the negative side in many essays by William Graham Sumner, whose attitude might be fairly expressed in the following paraphrase: Can anyone find an instance in all history where a nation set a goal to be attained, devised means for its attainment, applied those means, and reached that goal? It cannot be found. In his essay entitled "The Absurd Effort to Make the World Over," Sumner says: "Everyone of us is the child of his age and cannot get out of it. He is in the stream and is swept along with it. All his sciences and philosophy come to him out of it. Therefore the tide will not be changed by us. It will swallow up both us and our experiments. . . . That is why it

---

*Read before the Faculty Social Science Club, The University of Southern California, May, 1932.

[1]See "Tools and Culture," p. 72, and "Machines and Civilization," p. 84.

is the greatest folly of which a man is capable, to sit down with a slate and pencil to plan out a new social world."[2]

Herbert Spencer had previously declared that efforts on the part of man to direct the course of evolution, particularly by means of legislation, could only result in making things worse; to which Ward replied that the very fact that our efforts do make things worse is itself evidence that we are having *some* effect upon the course of social change. That gives room for encouragement, for we have only to acquire social wisdom in order to exert a *good* effect, thereby producing social progress.[3]

Ward's writings constitute a masterly refutation of Spencer and Sumner, as far as *theory* goes, but as a matter of *practice* societal self-direction along comprehensive and progressive lines has not occurred, either before or since, so far as I am able to show. Nevertheless societal self-direction is not only logically sound but ethically imperative when we consider the deplorable state of affairs on this planet, for in the present partial paralysis of civilization we behold the outcome of the policy of social drifting and *laissez faire*. It is true that there has been much social legislation and some social reconstruction, but all has been in the nature of piecemeal patchwork. Even worse, everything has been done with very partial vision, impelled by special interests in most cases, and uniformly without a comprehensive social purpose, goal, or plan.

Goal setting itself, although it presents the supreme test of individual and social intelligence, has no special organ in the case of even the most enlightened governments. The deliberative function is left to be exercised incidentally, in connection with special enterprises by private groups or legislative bodies. In fact, the larger plan and goal are treated as mere by-products of the special purposes. Meanwhile, "the shadow of the man on horseback" is seen by thinkers of high

---

[2]While I have searched Sumner's writings in vain in the effort to locate the passage above paraphrased, as I believe, from his words, it fairly represents his characteristic thought on this question. The essay quoted from is found in *War and Other Essays*, by William Graham Sumner (New Haven, 1911), edited by A. G. Keller.

[3]*Cf.* Oswald Spengler's essay entitled "The Sins of Legislators," in *Social Statics and Man versus the State;* also, Lester F. Ward, "The Political Ethics of Herbert Spencer," *Annals* of the American Academy of Political and Social Science, 4:582-619, 1894; and various other passages in the writings of both these authors.

ability, notably James Truslow Adams in his challenging
paper by that title[4] in a recent magazine. He shows with the
firm strokes of a master the steady decline in political sagacity
and integrity which has attended the course of popular self-
government from the days of Washington to the present hour.

If we may hope to advance through the present crisis and
guide our course *beyond civilization* into enlightenment and a
true collectivism worthy of humanity, some suggestion in the
way of method is called for just here. I therefore venture to
propose a *National Council on Social Goals and Welfare,*
whose function would be to determine the objects of social
striving in a detached and comprehensive way, analogous to
the deliberations and decisions of the United States Supreme
Court. Its decisions should be mandatory upon legislatures
to carry them out through statutes, and would constitute a
part of the supreme law of the land along with the decisions
of the Supreme Court itself. The principal difference would
be that, while the decrees of the Court deal with rights and
duties under existing law, and thus have to do with *order,*
the mandates of the Council would deal with relations under
laws that *ought to be* and would thus look toward the future
and *progress.* Its membership, chosen for long terms, or life
during good behavior, might be elected by occupational and
professional groupings representative of the dominant interests actually existing in the life of the people. Then the lower
house of Congress would rest on blocks of population, the
upper on territorial divisions, both as at present, and the
proposed deliberative and telic department, not now existent
in any form, would rest upon the vital interests of the people
themselves.

By such means we might avoid the dictatorship of the
men on horseback, on one hand, and the dictatorship of the
proletariat, on the other, by placing ourselves under the mandatory guidance of the elite, the "philosopher-statesmen" of
Plato's *Republic,* but here elected by the people, and charged
with the task of telling us where to set our goals, in the hope
of gaining what, in our better moments, we really want. This
is just what any person of character and purpose does with
his own life. He rouses himself, takes himself in hand, and

---

[4]James Truslow Adams, "Shadow of the Man on Horseback," *The
Atlantic Monthly,* 149:1-10, January, 1932.

dictates to himself. This means simply that his higher self dictates to his lower, in the sense that his more distant and all-inclusive purposes and his momentary impulses are both part of his own personality. The two are made, in such cases, to work together more harmoniously in the life of their common owner. This is done by compelling the impulses of the moment to subordinate themselves to the more comprehensive purposes determined upon in moments of reflection, and consigned to the will for execution. In a day when dictatorships of all shades are being either proposed or secretly desired, we here suggest one in which the people shall *dictate to themselves*, and by the same process through which an intelligent individual accomplishes that feat. The proposed National Council on Social Goals and Welfare would represent the higher and more rational aspect of the social or public mind, whose decrees would, by previous decision, have compelling authority over the more impulsive momentary impulses of that same collective mind as represented in the particular proposals and even projects of publicists and legislators, which represent only a partial and temporary movement of the national life.

The membership of the Council, functioning as the higher mind and purpose of the nation, would necessarily be composed of men and women representing various important social interests. It would include jurists, economists, sociologists, political scientists, philosophers, educators, artists, religious leaders, farmers, manufacturers, financiers, and others qualified to deal with the desired and desirable goals toward which the daily life and governmental policy of any people bent upon intelligent societal self-direction along progressive lines should be guided. Above all things, its deliberations and decisions should be placed above the reach of popular whim, passion, or obstruction. "Government by clamor" is increasing in the United States at an alarming rate. The "sovereign people" become more and more dictatorial toward not only elected legislators but even judges and grand juries, at the very time when its utter lack of discipline and social intelligence becomes more and more evident. It can hardly be stressed too strongly that we are facing a situation, in modern civilization, which has created at one stroke a more difficult economic and social order and less social maturity in the citizens for its management than the world has ever seen before. In other words, there never before existed on the earth so great a disparity between the social task and the social intelligence at hand to perform it. The tribal-minded social infant in conjunction with complicated machine civilization of planetary scope presents an incongruous combination full of grave portent for social progress. It seems reasonable to suggest that a civilized nation, especially one claiming to be highly enlightened, should take steps to exercise that same planful foresight which is believed to be the attribute of superior men, in the ordering of their private lives. Of course, we dare not ignore the immense weight of reasoning presented, notably in Professor Cooley's *Social Process*, to show that all living things, whether plants, persons, institutions, or nations, grow by a tentative, groping, trial-and-error method, always more or less unconscious in character.[5] Yet Cooley himself, after sapping most of the ground from beneath social telesis, could not refrain from adding a chapter on "Intelligence in Social Function," and another on "Rational Control Through Standards." Professor Ross also, after deprecating in his earlier writings the phrase "social progress" as hopelessly subjective, himself succumbed in a vigorous chapter on "Re-Shaping" in his *Principles of Sociology*, twenty and more years later. In similar fashion, Professor Keller seems to have yielded more fully to the seductions of societal self-direction during the interval between his *Societal Evolution* (1915) and his *Science of Society* (1927).

All this is significant of the power of this idea over the ablest sociological thinkers, even where logical defenses had been erected against it. And their experience is representative of the whole movement of popular and less strictly sociological thought during the last decade. At the very time when the notion of deliberately directed social progress was supposedly laid to rest in a decent academic grave, we have witnessed a flood of magazine articles, monographs, chapters, and textbooks on every aspect of the subject, old and new. Doubtless the horrors of World War I and the calamities that followed have forced the conviction that something better than aimless social drifting is indispensable if human life on this

---

[5] *Cf.* Charles Horton Cooley, *Social Process* (New York, 1918).

globe is to go forward. If this be wishful thinking, so much the better. All that is needed to make societal self-direction along progressive lines a feasible policy is the widespread practice of that kind of thinking on this subject among the masses of the people. Nothing stands in the way of an intelligent social order so much as the unintelligent apathy and social infantility of the citizens at large, and the first step toward something better is to *wish* for it more earnestly and more generally.

The plan suggested above is admittedly far fetched, if for no other reason than the fact that it is a product of detached reasoning on the problems of social progress. That in itself is alien to the prevailing temper. Among the intellectual, or rather the academic, classes it runs counter to the minutely analyzing, quantitatively measuring predilection of atomistic science.[6] Among the populace it would interrupt the preoccupation of the average man with his pursuit of immediate personal ends. Aside from the necessary struggle for daily bread, and its bastard offspring the insatiable greed of gain, the most important thing in life seems to be, for multitudes of men—and women—the obtaining of another smoke or another drink. Their astounding craving for the latter is driving multitudes to defy the statutes, dishonor the Constitution, and hobnob with low-lived bootleggers. By such lawless patronage they create a colossal fund on which thrives the murderous crew of hijackers, racketeers, and underworld professional thuggery in general.

Many who practice such inconsistencies deceive themselves with the notion that law and order can be trampled under foot at one time and place, yet held in honor at all others. Another chimera is the assumption that upon the legalization of alcoholic liquors all the army of organized lawlessness will meekly disband, leaving only the sporadic individual criminal

[6]Mechanistic tendencies aside, it may be regarded as even outside the limits of a broadly scientific sociology, if we correctly interpret the searching discussion of Professor Shenton, in which he concludes: "As sociology becomes more specifically a science of human association, the tendency will be to emphasize in applied sociology the ways and means of achieving proximate social ends. Such an emphasis, if it persists, will probably relegate to social philosophy the determination of comprehensive policies for the achievement of remote and as yet vaguely conceived ends."—Herbert N. Shenton, *The Practical Application of Sociology* (New York, 1927), p. 235.

to be dealt with, as in the days before crime assumed the proportions of a leading industry. This same unthinking attitude winked at terroristic night riding just after the World War, and has done likewise with gangster feuds in our great cities. The popular mind, which is essentially a child mind, seems unable to recognize the most hideous menaces against social welfare unless they chance to be dramatized in some unmistakable way such as happened to kidnaping when it invaded the Lindbergh nursery. Night riding, bootlegging, drunken driving, hijacking, racketeering, kidnaping—every one of these is a hideous social menace, a real bubonic plague or cancer, within the realm of social relations. But it is only the occasional citizen who shows any clear understanding of their deadly menace to all that decent men hold dear. When one reflects that our colonial forerunners understood such things and many more that are hidden from the social intelligence of their politically degenerate successors today, it is immensely disconcerting to our present effort at vindicating the capacity of the people to direct the course of social change toward soundly conceived goals of general welfare. There is involved in this the problem of social infantility and social age, which I cannot take space to develop here, although I have tried to discuss it elsewhere.[7] It tends more and more to disclose itself as the principal hindrance to societal self-direction, acute but happily not incurable. As I understand it, the social infant is a grownup of normal body and mind who has carried his nursery attitudes over into adult life, especially the selfishness that marks the infant. In persons of normal social development this gives place, more or less fully, to a sense of the claims and welfare of others. Social age thus means growth in the socialized disposition. In a vital sense it is the altruistic *human nature* which is fostered in primary groups. Individuals vary in the degree to which they attain it. The governing factor lies in the intimate primary-group life, although for more mature intellectual persons there is much power in the appeal of moral and social idealism. At any rate social infantility is apparently not incurable, so that

---

[7] In *Social Process and Human Progress*, Chap. VII, "Social Age as a Key to Progress," Chap. VIII, "The Social Infant and the Imbecile Group," Chap. IX, "Youth and Social Progress." [Also discussed in the first two essays of this book.]

even for the swarming millions of grown-up babies that frolic in the pathway of social progress much might be done by proper treatment of a moral and social nature.

As for our National Council on Social Goals and Welfare, it is perfectly easy to raise a swarm of objections bearing upon its practicality, such as the method of selecting the members; the probable refusal of Congress to enact the legislation required to render its decrees effective; or even the likelihood that the people would nullify them as they have the prohibition laws. With the public mind on its present childish level, such objections are not easily answered. Herbert Spencer was eternally right when he said, "There is no political alchemy by which it is possible to get golden conduct out of leaden instincts." Modern life, especially in the giant city, which is its perfect symbol, with its overspeeded mobility, its superficial secondary contacts, its anonymity, individualism, selfish pursuit of pleasurable new experience, and thirst for social recognition of a frothy sort, has more of lead than gold in its make-up. And back of it all stands the all-important fact that the *spiritual community*, uniting men with God and to one another in a deep sense of the sacredness and eternal significance of life, of duty and devotion toward values immeasurably bigger than one's busy little self, or even a whole life spent measuring itself by itself—that this community has been immensely reduced by the growth and dissemination of a materialistic and mechanistic philosophy of life.

It is coming to be quite widely realized that the breakdown in modern life centers in the *human* factor. The two things just described, namely, the failure of the far-ranging, swiftly moving modern mode of life to develop socialized persons of mature social age, and the decline of the spiritual community, account largely for that breakdown. In such cases the shortcoming is moral and spiritual. Alongside this we see an *intellectual* inadequacy in the fact that, with the whole world languishing in unparalleled depression and perplexity, no man or group of men seems able to explain its cause or to apply a remedy. Of those most responsible—the financiers, industrialists, and economists—only a very few have spoken boldly; and their pronouncements, aside from painful inadequacy, yield mainly a confusion of voices. The plain truth is that our machine-made economic world is too big for our intellects, even those of the best. Plenty of "leaders" have shown themselves adept at exploiting the world economy for personal gain, and at aggravating its evils, but utterly unable to explain or control it except in the partial and selfish manner all too familiar in the life of individuals and nations. Here again we know in part and we prophesy in part, seeing only through a glass darkly—perhaps none so darkly as those who insist on the nation's entering more and more deeply into the affairs of world *economy* while at the same time drawing more and more selfishly away from the world *community*, which alone can make that economy effective and of benefit to mankind through an interchange of common ideals as well as material goods. Here again the human factor as such proves to be the root of the trouble—ancient tribal mind dabbling blindly in cosmopolitan matters far beyond its depth.

In all these things the causal factor is sufficiently evident to suggest the remedy, albeit only in general terms. The way of deliverance lies in a world-wide movement aimed at the re-evaluation of life. The growing conviction that neither science nor machines can save us constitutes a long stride in the right direction. Here is opportunity for a new crusade that might engage and satisfy the idealistic spirit of youth as marching for beer[8] can never do it. Judge Lester Roth has recently suggested[9] that the growth of crime in the United States may be explained by the fact that "the last frontier has been crossed." For the first time in history "The call of strange scenes and things that lie beyond the far-off haze is destined no longer to thrill the imagination of the daring." His thesis is suggested by the subtitle of his article: "Has the spirit of the old frontier turned lawless?" Judge Roth recognizes the field for adventurous spirits that still remains unexplored in the depths of the sea and in the air, but holds that they offer "outlets for a comparative few." The whole hypothesis is brilliant and ably presented, but the author neglects the most promising frontier left for adventurous spirits —the struggle for a new social order. That way lies a new crusade which has been left thus far largely to the dis-

---

[8]Reference here is to the new "crusaders," as they sacrilegiously name their militant liquor campaign.

[9]*Cf.* Judge Lester Roth, "Criminals or Adventurers?" *Los Angeles Times Sunday Magazine*, May 22, 1932.

inherited, impelled by that deep sense of injustice which makes
the goal process of Equalization as relentless in the long run
as Utilization[10] itself. For those historical materialists who
think that the last named is the only process that is grounded
in the basic facts of nature and life are misled by superficial
analysis. One thing that can be said of all living things is
that they are interested in themselves in the sense that they
are self-biased, as Professor Perry has abundantly shown.[11]
They must be so or perish, because life is always a precarious
enterprise in the cosmos as constituted. It is because of this
that the process of Utilization is inseparable from the life
process itself, as everybody is able to understand. But the
process of Equalization (which always means here the equalization of opportunity, and not any effort at dead-levelism) is
equally rooted in precisely the same thing, and that is the
prime necessity of discriminating, selective behavior on the
part of every life-loving creature. For every such being has
sooner or later to learn that there are similar beings animated
with the same primordial self-perpetuating interest who, if
ruthlessly ignored, will become in themselves a hostile and
active part of an already precarious environment. In other
words, the same primordial life force which, through self-
interest, begets the ruthless aggressor raises up also the im-
movable resisters. As for the Evaluation process, instead of
figuring as an afterthought and an ornamental aspect of the
world, it was present when the lowest foundations of life itself
were laid. It exists in our very premise, namely, that all
values are at bottom simply the *discriminations* and *selections*
of self-biased, that is to say living, beings.

The past and the future are ever united in the present.
Consequently, as Professor Bouglé has finely phrased it, "One
reforms only the given; one works only upon history. This
is why the prime condition of all progress is always a tradition."[12] This is grandly true, but equally true is it, as sociologists also have pointed out, that "when a community has rejected the old traditions there is no direct way back to them.

---

[10]For the sociological significance of the terms Utilization, Equalization, and Evaluation, see Clarence M. Case, *Social Process and Human
Progress* (New York, 1931), pp. 61-71.

[11]Ralph Barton Perry, *The Moral Economy* (New York, 1909).

[12]*Cf.* C. Bouglé, *The Evolution of Values* (Helen Stalker Sellars' translation; New York, 1926), p. 39.

It must recreate what it cannot restore."[13] Thus the old values
have to be restated, perhaps with the very same content, but
with different symbols, from age to age, as the epochs of
history arise.

Returning to the specific theme, the two great goal processes
which I have called Equalization and Evaluation offer a vast,
almost unexplored field for the adventurous spirit, imagination, and idealism of youth. Many heads are being broken
every day on that frontier, and many social scalps will yet be
taken. In fact, it is the most promising field for new experience now accessible to human adventure, and it presents the
best answer to Professor William James' call for "a moral
equivalent for war." In a world-wide youth movement across
the frontiers of social and international idealism lies the
greatest hope of humanity, and it is the great task of education and religion, in a word, religious education in a bigger
and bolder sense than now exists, to bring about the march
beyond civilization.

The particular direction which such a movement should
take is fairly clear, for many are already on the way. One
of these tendencies is a deliberate repudiation of the giant
city as an evil to be deliberately avoided. Twenty years ago
Viscount James Bryce set forth seven "reasons why a great
city is a great evil."[14] During the two succeeding decades the
menace of the overgrown cities has waxed worse, and they
have now found in Oswald Spengler's great chapter on "The
Soul of the City"[15] a word artist capable of portraying with
adequate power their stupendous good and evil alike. It is
the giant, overgrown city, the *megalopolis,* that is referred to
here. The ecological and technical reasons that once justified
it hold true no longer, having been set aside by high-voltage
power lines and truck highways. Economically it has passed
the point of diminishing returns. Until a certain magnitude
is attained, the city serves as the hospitable hearth of the
finest aspects of the higher cultures; but beyond that point,

---

[13]Robert M. MacIver, *Community,* as quoted in Emory S. Bogardus,
Contemporary Sociology (Los Angeles, 1931), p. 316.

[14]Number 20 in *National Housing Association Publications* (New
York, 1913), as quoted in Clarence Marsh Case, *Outlines of Introductory
Sociology* (New York, 1924), pp. 707 ff.

[15]Oswald Spengler, *The Decline of the West* (New York, 1929), Vol.
II, Chap. IV.

it becomes a consuming furnace for culture itself considered as a fit abiding place for the human spirit. Just now many are turning away from it and going back to the land. The movement should be encouraged, and every other possible means used to keep the city within bounds or, better, to scatter it into garden cities. Like the machine, of which it is the final expression, the giant city is a real monstrosity when not controlled by human idealism. Along with all mechanism, it is a good servant but a very bad master. Only when the spirit of the living creature is lifted up can the wheels be lifted up; and only as the spirit of the living creature goes forward will the wheels go forward, as Ezekiel, with prophetic vision, so perfectly portrayed the truth as it is, both then, and now, and always.[16]

It may turn out that neither the rural peasant countryside nor the giant city is the form for the future, but something between the two. This is the villa of ancient times and the so-called "rurban" economy of contemporary American rural sociologists. The latter were driven to coin that word because they found themselves facing a kind of life which was neither *rural* nor *urban*, but which blended the characteristics of both, exactly as the new term itself combines the two older words. The whole of southern California, with the possible exception of a very few extremely isolated sections of the mountains and the desert, is a rural-urban, or *rurban*, community. And even those remote spots seem destined to be caught up by the main stream of life under the rapid extension of highways, telephones, and privately installed radio receiving sets. If this movement continues, it may prove the solution of the present problem, to the extent that it is a national one, although at that it will have to operate in the face of the even more difficult problem of world economy and international trade. But leaving that aside for the present, and proceeding upon the principle that one should first attempt to set his own national house in order, the present movement back to the land may possibly mark a turning point in Western history. It is now remarked among the sociologists, particularly those of the ecological school, that *space* in the geographic sense has been practically eliminated as an important factor

---

[16]Ezek. 1:15-21.

in community life. It has been translated by applied science, in a word, the machine, into questions of *time* and *social distance*. This completely revolutionizes the problem of country life upon its social side, leaving the possibility of a satisfying existence there squarely up to economic theory and practice. The sociological analysis itself has been under way for a quarter of a century, beginning with the inauguration of the Country Life Movement in 1907. Professor G. Walter Fiske pointed out, in 1916, "two parallel processes developing rather noticeably, the socializing and the urbanizing of country life."[17] Socialization, in his terminology, was "a civilizing process" in which individuals grow into a community of purpose and efficient cooperative action. By "urbanization" he denoted "the spread of the social ideals and customs of the city." This he regarded as a detriment to country life, whereas socialization promised to solve many problems of rural sociology.

Since those words were written the situation has changed. The mail-order catalogue, which he mentioned as a potent factor, has been enormously supplemented with the automobile highway, telephone, airplane, and radio, so that there is no stemming the invasion of the rural districts by city modes of life. This urbanization, and not socialization as he defined it, is the "civilizing process," which has been traced elsewhere by the present writer[18] as the depersonalization and mechanization of life. The truth is that the city is suffering from it also, and has in "urbanization" merely infected the country with its own malady, which is civilization itself. But in the movement of population back to the land, the possibility of a remedy appears. Let the tide of living beings follow their civilized machine patterns out from the city into the open country, and the more disgusted and weary they are with the crowding, the din, and the superficial social racing of metropolitan existence, the more disposed they may be to help in building a finely socialized community life, mentally and spiritually united while dispersed throughout the land, in the daily presence of that natural beauty and comparative solitude which have always held a deep and abiding appeal for

---

[17]In *Publications of the American Sociological Society*, 11:56-61.
[18]See the essay in this volume entitled, "Machines and Civilization."

the human heart. In the degree that this turns out to be *villa* life its occupational and industrial base will still be the city, with partial expression in the countryside. Its extension beyond the villa zone depends upon our ability to master the economic problems of farming and other occupations of country life. But whatever its extent, the essential factor will be modern methods of transportation and communication brought into the service of truly human and genuinely social ideals; and thus by the union of men and machines under the guidance of social telesis a new kind of community, combining the best features of country and town, may even yet be achieved.

Another road to a less civilized and a better human world lies equally plain before us, and that is some comprehensive arrangement for the redistribution of wealth. A thorough and sweeping plan of social insurance, beginning with unemployment and including provision for old age, offers probably the best method. It has the merit of being adequate without being radical, inasmuch as it limits the "rights" of private property without abolishing it. But all that is a matter of detail in the field of method.[19] Without quibbling over ways and means, we need to recognize the all-important basic truth that no real and lasting prosperity can be expected in any land where the purchasing, and hence consuming, power of the great mass of the laboring people is kept so far below that which, on the basis of their proportionate number, they would naturally be expected to consume. These are elementary truths of social justice which cannot be gainsaid in the name of economic theory, for all such theory is merely a human interpretation of human evaluations colored by the existing institutional situation, as Professor Cooley's incomparable chapter on "The Sphere of Pecuniary Evaluation" clearly shows.[20] Economic theory lies closer to forensic and literary art than to natural law, and much of it can safely be laid aside like any other outworn body of dogma or interpretation.

---

[19]The important thing for our present discussion is to note the general truth that some such reform is required in order (1) to reduce the grotesque inequalities in the distribution of wealth regarded as a mere matter of difference in the objective, physical sense, and to remove the unnecessary anxiety of the poor; (2) to allay the sense of injustice that inevitably accompanies such inequalities; (3) to rescue democracy and social idealism from the *deadly menace that lurks* in such things.

[20]Charles H. Cooley, *Social Process* (New York, 1918), Chap XXVII.

The fact that orthodox economics assumes the existing institutions of private property and the wage system as a datum for all its reasonings is sufficient proof of its merely *provisional* character, even if it were not already challenged by the new "welfare economics" within its own camp. In spite of its present disorganization, human nature may have possibilities within itself which must leave much of economic theory high and dry along with the machine-ridden world it is now preparing to leave behind, if the hope of a future beyond civilization is not destined to fail.

"Beyond civilization" does not, of course, mean that we are going to be so foolish as to wreck all the machines or turn our backs upon them. It means simply that they must come under the rational power which resides in men, amidst all their infantilities and follies, to perceive their larger common interest and compose their minor differences in order to attain it. Upon this distinctly human trait, most clearly portrayed by William Graham Sumner,[21] rests the possibility of societal self-direction within nations and between them. A new world order is emerging at Geneva through the heartbreaking strivings of those who are welding a World League in the very furnace of tribulation. Perhaps by means of it the spirit of humanity someday not only will reduce and curb the war machine but will prove itself able to master the machine economy itself. Furthermore, such rational control of it might make possible the world-wide diffusion, not of the *universal culture scheme*, since the tribes of earth all possess it in their own right and heritage, but of such technical modification of it as is calculated to benefit all mankind. This would include improved methods of transportation and communication, hygiene and sanitation, and other nature techniques, along with such ideologies and idealisms as democracy, equality of the sexes, international cooperation, world peace, and any other culture patterns that possess appeal and benefit for human beings everywhere. If, upon that common basic scheme, the tribes of earth could rear the rich patterns of their own national cultures, mankind might pass, by virtue of the machine itself, beyond civilization into a new era of true enlightenment. In this we do not accept the doom pro-

---

[21] *Folkways*, p. 18 *et passim;* also in his *War and Other Essays*, edited by A. G. Keller, Essay One.

nounced by the great Spengler, who conceives of historical cultures as living beings, each with its own unique organization of values which perish with it when its life cycle is completed. The point of view herein attempted is less imaginative and mystical, hence more prosaic. It is also more cheerful, if not more practicable, taking account of the universal culture scheme of Wissler as outlined in his *Man and Culture*. That scheme suggests an underlying unity in the cultures of all mankind, and a common stock or stem upon which might be engrafted whatever benefits machine civilization has really won when tested by universal human values. Along with this we have to recognize that not one of those historic cultures whose uniqueness so enthralls Spengler was developed in isolation. The recent researches of ethnologists into culture history have revealed an astonishing amount of culture contact and diffusion as far back as our knowledge of the Ancient World is able to penetrate. In consequence, the conclusion is that about nine parts of any culture is borrowed where one part is originated. This is especially true of the great world cultures—Indian, Babylonian, Arabian, Egyptian, Greek, Roman, and European—described in Spengler's *The Decline of the West*. It should be said of them, as it was of men, that "none liveth to itself and none dieth to itself." This is true because of the historic fact that culture, like the fabled Phoenix bird, rises always out of its own ashes. As Spengler himself admits, the *race* continues (in his phraseology, the *blood triumphs*), and by the same token culture continues, since men have never been found existing without culture. The particular values and patterns which appeal so strongly to the artistic soul, as in Spengler pre-eminently, do die down and perish, but out of the primordial and ever-living root new culture stems arise and flourish, somewhat as one may behold, in the great groves of California, a *family tree* not dead but ever living, namely, the *Sequoia sempervirens*, whose overlapping generations spring out of one single rootage, and endure, as it were a single tree, for unnumbered generations.*

---

*Reprinted from *Sociology and Social Research*, 17:117-36, November-December, 1932.

CREATIVE PEACEMAKING*

1. War and peace are two related aspects of a single social process, called "synergy" by Lester F. Ward.[1] Under that term he referred to the cosmic process, defined by him as "the harmonious and constructive working together of the anti-thetical forces of nature." Simmel[2] shows that war does not end just when the armistice begins; if the movement toward peace had not already begun, the armistice could not have been arranged. Likewise, preparations for war begin during peace; otherwise, war could not equip itself sufficiently to interrupt peace so suddenly.

Sumner,[3] Giddings,[4] and Novicow[5] have all shown that peace is a way of living together through mutually advantageous cooperation (called "exchange" by Novicow), whereas war is the interruption of those arrangements by appeal to force. As Ward has pointed out, force is essentially unintelligent and destructive, whereas the "method of indirection," or reason, is the only truly progressive principle and method. He completely refuted all the ruinous nonsense of the propaganda of the deed" in labor conflicts and of "total war frightfulness" long before its mad claims were extended to national and international affairs.

2. A long line of eminent thinkers (George Fox, Sully, William Penn, Sumner, Giddings, Norman Angell, President Kingdon) have clearly demonstrated an ever-working social process which results in "the enlargement of the peace group" through the growing perception of a larger common interest

---

*Summary of a talk delivered from an outline before the Annual Meeting of the Pacific Sociological Society, December 29-30, 1941.

[1]Lester F. Ward, *Dynamic Sociology* (New York and London, 1883), Vol. II, pp. 95-102, 308-99, *et passim; Pure Sociology* (New York and London, 1903), pp. 171 ff.; *Applied Sociology* (Boston, 1906), pp. 331-39.

[2]Georg Simmel, "The Sociology of Conflict, III," *American Journal of Sociology*, 9:798-811, 1904. See also Nicholas J. Spykman, *The Social Theory of Georg Simmel* (Chicago, 1925), pp. 112-13, 125-27.

[3]William G. Sumner, *War and Other Essays*, ed. E. G. Keller (New Haven, 1911), pp. 3-40.

[4]Franklin H. Giddings, *Democracy and Empire* (New York, 1900), Chap. XX, "The Gospel of Non-Resistance," pp. 343-57.

[5]Jacques Novicow, *The Mechanism and Limits of Human Association: The Foundations of a Sociology of Peace*, translated by Sophia Hersch Otis in *American Journal of Sociology*, 23:289-349, 1917.

which always underlies particular conflicts. They are thus actually treating, in general terms, the process of social synergy, called "accommodation" in the field of sociology. Its two basic processes I shall designate as opposition and cooperation, defining them as follows: Opposition is that social process in which persons or groups move toward ends that are nonsharable or incompatible. Cooperation is that social process in which persons or groups move toward ends that are sharable or compatible.

The basic assumption of these definitions is that, normally, human beings fight for ends and not for the sake of fighting, or, as Cooley aptly put it, "we injure one another more often with our elbows than we do with our fists." The exception might be the relatively few quarrelsome trouble hunters and would-be dominators, the *militaristic* as distinguished from the *militant* type.

3. Responsibility for current wars is immensely complex and is widely distributed. Nietzsche, Treitschke, Bernhardi, Machiavelli; the militarists, militants, interventionists, isolationists, League of Nations bolters, anti-League progressive disarmament advocates—all these and other groups have partly, often unwittingly and unintentionally, helped to create the present ghastly situation; in short, all those who permitted world economy to outrun world community.

4. Among the creative peacemakers are Sully with his *Grand Design of Henry IV;* Penn with his *Plan for the Peace of Europe;* Wilson with his "Fourteen Points" and the League of Nations; Root with his World Court; Kingdon with his prize essay, "The Price of Peace"; Streit with his *Union Now;* Roosevelt and Churchill with their "Atlantic Charter"; and the now existent, salvaged League itself—and everybody who is dedicated to living creatively, by the method of rational indirection, and who promotes the welfare of the world by creating and organizing order, law, justice, and peace.*

---

*Reprinted by permission from *Proceedings of the Pacific Sociological Society*, Research Studies of the State College of Washington, Vol. X, No. 1, pp. 17-18, March, 1942.

COMPLETE LIST OF THE PUBLISHED WRITINGS OF CLARENCE MARSH CASE

(Prepared by John Eric Nordskog)

Twenty-four poems of nature and social relations, in the *Indianapolis Journal, Indianapolis Press, Boston Transcript, The American Friend* (Philadelphia), Noblesville (Indiana) *High School Autocrat*, and the *Earlhamite* (Earlham College); 1897-1906.

"The Latest Science (Sociology) and Christianity," "Social Science and Christianity," "War Opposed from a Worldly Standpoint," "Principles Toward a Solution of the Liquor Problem," "The Church and the Meeting House," "Some Aspects of Education," and related articles, in *The American Friend*, volumes published from 1898 to 1908.

The Banner of the White Horse. A Tale of the Saxon Conquest. New York: Charles Scribner's Sons, 1916. Pp. 235.

"Religion and the Concept of Progress," *Journal of Religion*, 1:160-73, March, 1921.

"Dilemma of Social Religion," *ibid.*, 2:277-90, May, 1922.

"Instinctive and Cultural Factors in Group Conflicts," *The American Journal of Sociology*, 28:1-20, July, 1922.

"Eugenics as a Social Philosophy," *Journal of Applied Sociology*, 7:1-12, September-October, 1922.

Non-Violent Coercion. A Study in Methods of Social Pressure. New York and London: The Century Company, 1923. Pp. 423.

"Gandhi and the Indian National Mind. A Fragment and a Suggestion," *Journal of Applied Sociology*, 7:293-301, July-August, 1923.

Outlines of Introductory Sociology: A Textbook of Readings in Social Science. New York: Harcourt, Brace and Company, 1924. Pp. 980.

"The Culture Concept in Social Science," *Journal of Applied Sociology*, 8:146-55, January-February, 1924.

"What Is a Social Problem?" *ibid.*, 8:268-73, May-June, 1924.

"Durkheim's Educational Sociology," *ibid.*, 9:30-33, September-October, 1924.

"Conflict and Cooperation in Social Progress," *ibid.*, 9:179-86, January-February, 1925.

"Clarence E. Rainwater: 1884-1925," *ibid.*, 10:22-24, September-October, 1925.

"What Is Social Progress?" *ibid.*, 10:109-19, November-December, 1925.

"Present Position of Sociology in Germany," by Andreas Walter, translated by Clarence Marsh Case and Margaret Graham Borthwick, *ibid.*, 10:229-38, January-February, 1926.

"Sumner of Yale," *ibid.*, 10:418-21, May-June, 1926.

"The Sociology of Clarence E. Rainwater," *ibid.*, 10:507-16, July-August, 1926.

Sociology of Religion. Syllabus. Los Angeles: The University of Southern California, 1926-27. Pp. 58. Mimeographed. Out of print.

"Method in the Social Sciences," *ibid.*, 11:255-65, January-February, 1927.

"Culture as a Distinctive Human Trait," *The American Journal of Sociology*, 32:906-20, May, 1927.

"A Crisis in Anthropological Research," *Sociology and Social Research*, 12:26-34, September-October, 1927.

"What Is Social Research?" *ibid.*, 12:132-36, November-December, 1927.

"Social Imbecility and Social Age," *ibid.*, 12:218-42, January-February, 1928.

"Scholarship in Sociology," *ibid.*, 12:323-40, March-April, 1928.

"A Challenge to Western Culture," *ibid.*, 12:414-20, May-June, 1928.

"A Landmark in Sociological Literature," *ibid.*, 13:133-39, November-December, 1928.

"René Worms: An Appreciation," by Clarence Marsh Case and Fred Woerner, *ibid.*, 13:403-25, May-June, 1929.

"A New Kind of Community Study," *ibid.*, 14:25-29, September-October, 1929.

"Toward Gestalt Sociology," *ibid.*, 15:3-27, September-October, 1930.

Social Process and Human Progress. New York: Harcourt, Brace and Company, 1931. Pp. 336.

"Engineers and Social Progress," *Sociology and Social Research*, 15:451-55, May-June, 1931.

Readings in Ethnology. Los Angeles: The University of Southern California, 1931. Pp. 326. Mimeographed. Out of print.

"Tools and Culture," *The Personalist*, 13:245-60, October, 1932.

"Beyond Civilization," *Sociology and Social Research*, 17:117-36, November-December. 1932.

"Machines and Civilization," *The Personalist*, 14:11-30, January, 1933.

"Technocracy and Social Engineering," *Sociology and Social Research,* 17:331-39, March-April, 1933.

"Note on the Documentation of Social Research," *ibid.,* 17:396-97, March-April, 1933.

"Leadership and Conjuncture: A Sociological Hypothesis," *ibid.,* 17:510-13, July-August, 1933.

"Closing In on the Machine," *ibid.,* 19:210-17, January-February, 1935.

"The Cave Man Started This Depression," *ibid.,* 20:8-17, September-October, 1935.

"Friends and Social Thinking," in *Beyond Dilemmas; Quakers Look at Life,* S. C. Laughlin, editor. New York, Philadelphia, etc.: J. B. Lippincott Company, 1937, pp. 125-51.

"An Old-Age Pension for Young People," *Sociology and Social Research,* 22:14-20, September-October, 1937.

"The Social Infant on the Road," *ibid.,* 23:3-17, September-October, 1938.

"The Value Concept in Sociology and Related Fields," *ibid.,* 23:403-30, May-June, 1939.

"Creative Peacemaking," *Proceedings of the Pacific Sociological Society.* Research Studies of the State College of Washington, Vol. X, No. 1, March, 1942. Pullman: State College of Washington, 1942, pp. 17-18.

"A Tentative Social Age Trend Chart," printed for the first time in this book of essays, 1944, pp. 9-22.

INDEX